Starfish K2
Student's Book

```
    ┌─ Catalogue Publication Data ─────────┐
    │ *Starfish K2 Student's Book*         │
    │ Author: Paul Drury                   │
    │ Pearson Educación de México, S.A. de C.V., 2019 │
    │ ISBN: 978-607-32-4665-1              │
    │ Area: ELT                            │
    │ Format: 30.5 x 23.5 cm   Page count: 248 │
    └──────────────────────────────────────┘
```

Managing Director: Sergio Fonseca ■ **Innovation & Learning Delivery Director:** Alan David Palau ■ **Regional Content Manager - English:** Andrew Starling ■ **Innovation and Implementation Manager:** Gonzalo Pastor ■ **Publisher:** Hened Manzur ■ **Content Development:** Miroslava Guerra ■ **Content Support:** Susana Moreno ■ **Art and Design Coordinator:** Juan Manuel Santamaría ■ **Design Process Supervisor:** Salvador Pereira ■ **Layout:** Berenice Hinojosa ■ **Cover Design:** BrandB/Fenómeno ■ **Interior Design:** BrandB/Fenómeno ■ **Photo Research:** Salvador Pereira ■ **Photo Credits:** Shutterstock ■ **Illustrations:** Ana Elena García, Belén García Monroy, Gerardo Sánchez, Miguel Angel Chávez, Herenia González, Ismael Vázquez, José de Santiago Torices, Luz Yéspiz, Marcela Gómez, Olivia González, Sheila Cabeza de Vaca, Víctor Sandoval, Ximena García Trigos

The Publisher wishes to acknowledge the valuable collaboration of **Sophie Angerman**, author of the Mathematics program.

© Pearson Educación de México, S.A. de C.V., 2019

First published, 2019

ISBN PRINT BOOK: 978-607-32-4665-1

D.R. © 2019 por Pearson Educación de México, S.A. de C.V.
Avenida Antonio Dovalí Jaime #70
Torre B, Piso 6, Colonia Zedec Ed. Plaza Santa Fe
Delegación Álvaro Obregón, México, Ciudad de México, C. P. 01210

Esta obra se terminó de imprimir en enero del 2023, en los talleres de Servicios Profesionales de Impresión S.A. de C.V. Calle Mimosas 31, Col. Santa María Insurgentes, C. P. 06430 México, CDMX

www.pearsonelt.com

Impreso en México. *Printed in Mexico.*

1 2 3 4 5 6 7 8 9 0 - 22 21 20 19

All rights reserved. No part of this publication may be reproduced, stored in a retrieval system, or transmitted in any form or by any means, electronic, mechanical, photocopying, recording, or otherwise, without the prior permission of the publisher.

Pearson Hispanoamérica
Argentina ■ Belice ■ Bolivia ■ Chile ■ Colombia ■ Costa Rica ■ Cuba ■ República Dominicana ■ Ecuador ■ El Salvador ■ Guatemala ■ Honduras ■ México ■ Nicaragua ■ Panamá ■ Paraguay ■ Perú ■ Uruguay ■ Venezuela

Contents

Unit		Page
1	What do you like about yourself?	4
2	Why do we go to school?	29
3	How can you help your family at home?	54
4	Why do you feel hot or cold?	79
5	What other living things are around us?	116
6	Why is food important?	141
7	How can farm animals help us?	178
8	Who lives and works in my town?	203

- **Look at the pictures and say what the story is about.**

- **Listen. Circle the children that look similar.** 🎧 ✏️

- **Color and talk about yourself.**

My hair is

My eyes are

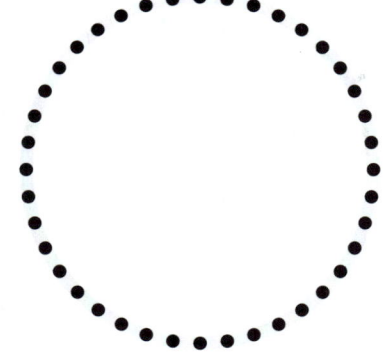

Objectives: Listen to and understand a story.

Unit 1

5

● **Listen. Color the pictures that start with *a*. Trace.**

Phonemic Awareness
Learning to Know

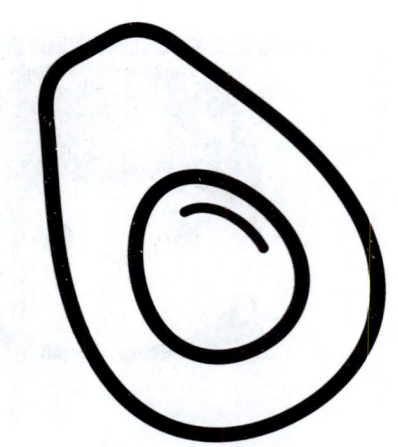

Unit 1

Objectives: Identify the short /a/ vowel sound.

Name, color, and match.

Mathematical Thinking
Learning to Know

Objectives: Name basic shapes.

Unit 1

7

- **Draw yourself and a family member.**

Language Instruction and Communication
Learning to Know

Me

My _____

- **Tell a partner about yourself and a family member.**

Think! Who has similar hair in your family?

8　Unit 1

Objectives: Use target language to talk about physical characteristics.

- **Look and listen. Circle the correct child.**

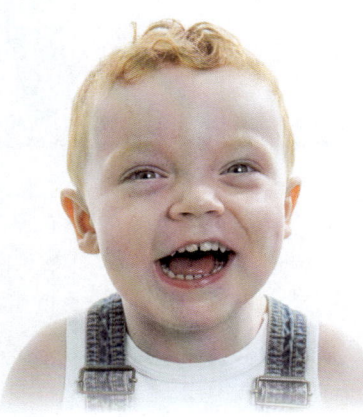 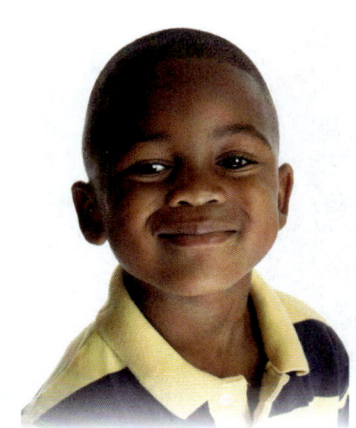

Think!
Does everyone in your family look similar to you?

- **Circle the child who looks most like you.**

Unit 1

Objectives: Learn about and compare facial features.

- Listen and order the pictures.

- Tell a partner what you like about yourself.

Unit 1

Objectives: Learn why it is important to like yourself.

- **Listen. Circle the funny hair.**

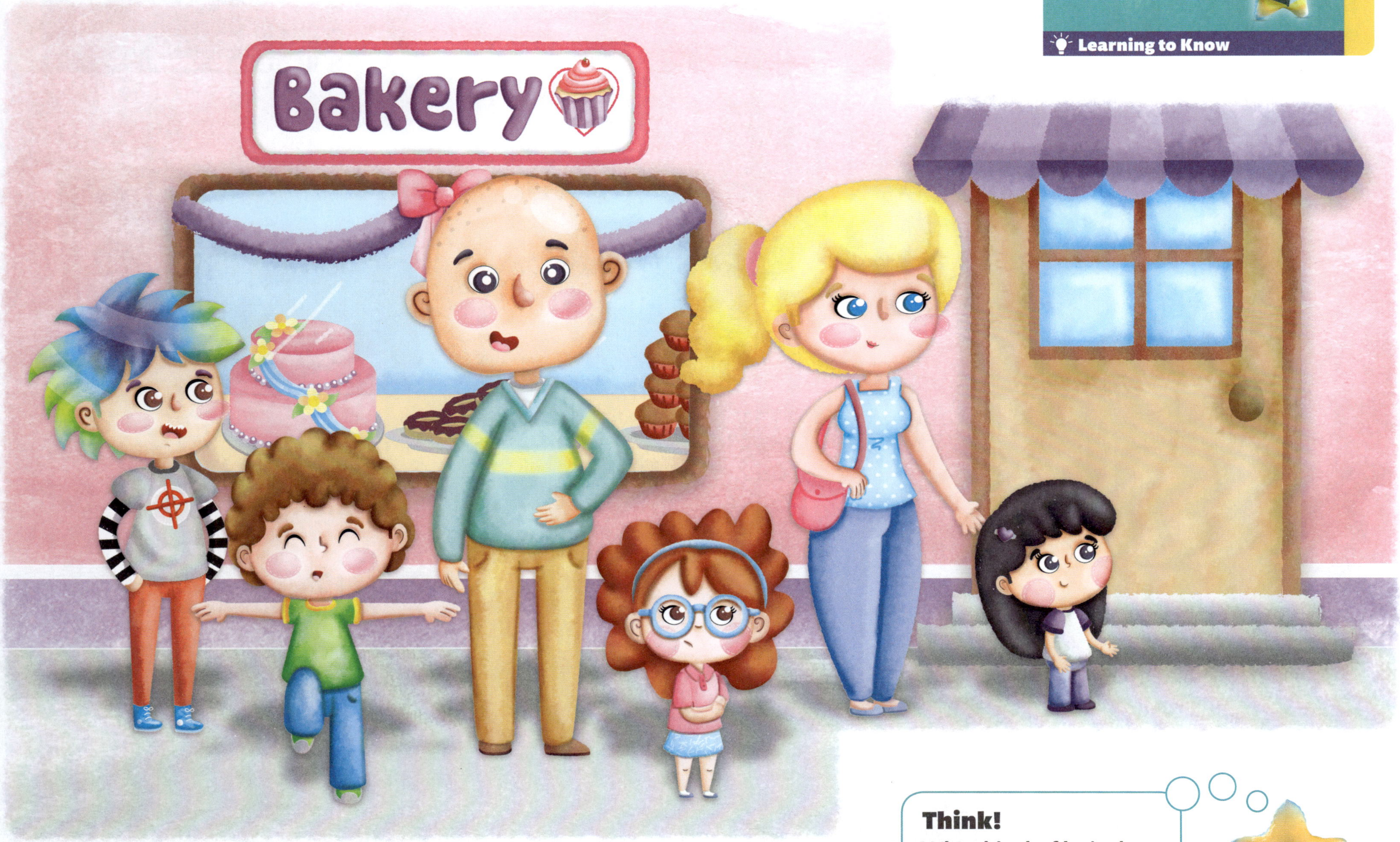

- **Listen and say the poem.**

Think!
What kind of hair does your teacher have?

Objectives: Listen to, understand, and retell a poem about different types of hair.

Unit 1

- **Listen. Circle the pictures that start with e. Trace.**

Phonemic Awareness
Learning to Know

Unit 1

Objective: Identify the short /e/ vowel sound.

Write numbers. Count and color.

Mathematical Thinking

Learning to Know

5

6

7

8

9

Objectives: Trace and write numbers.
Match numbers and objects up to 9.

Unit 1

● **Listen and match.**

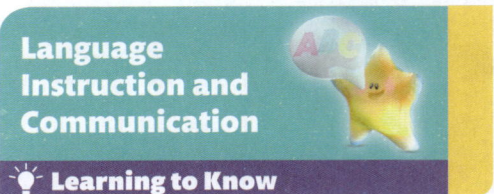

 Marian

 Tommy

 Lisa

Think! Can you change the color of your hair? How?

● **Choose a picture and tell a friend.**

Objectives: Use target language to compare different types of hair.

Make a wig.

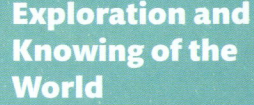

Exploration and Knowing of the World

✋ Learning to Do

Think!
Can you take your hair off?
How can you change your hair?

Play a game using wigs.

Objectives: Learn about and compare different types of hair (curly, straight, wavy).

Unit 1

● **Look and draw a happy or a sad face.**

Personal, Social, and Emotional Development

♡ Learning to Live Together
Learning to Live with Others

Think!
What can happen if you don't wash your hands before you eat?

Objectives: Take care of and respect themselves.

- **Listen and sing. Circle the children with long hair.**

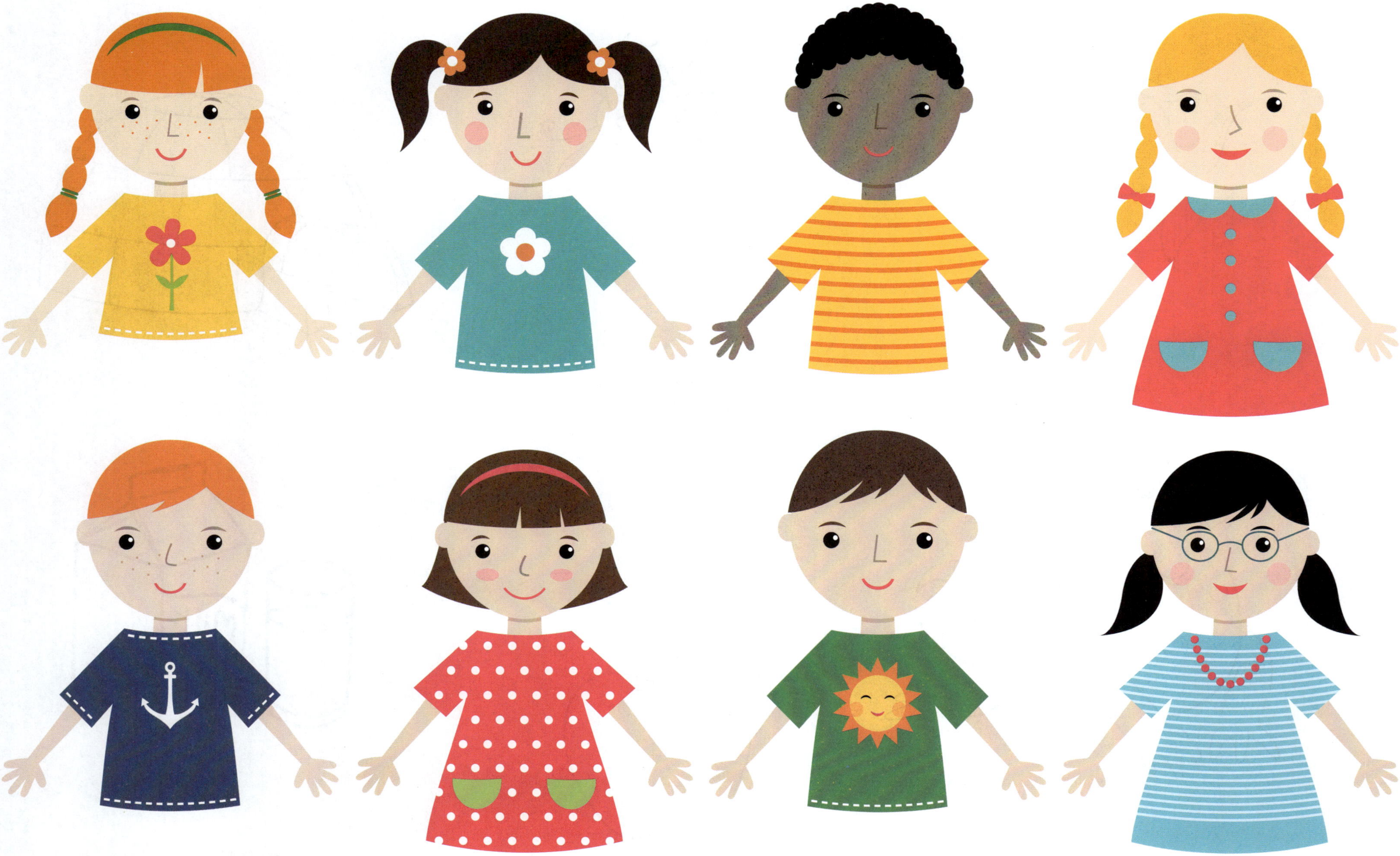

Objectives: Listen to, understand, and sing a song about what children like about themselves.

Unit 1

Listen. Color the words with a short *i* sound. Trace.

Phonemic Awareness
Learning to Know

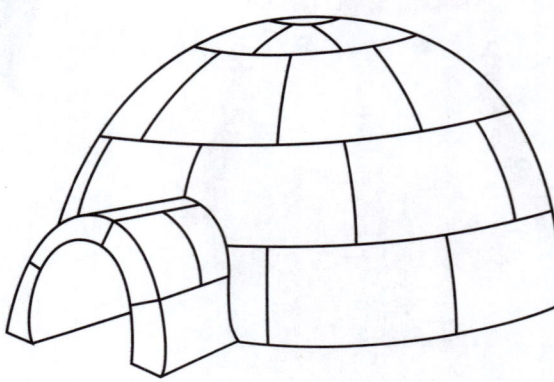

i

Objectives: Identify words with the short /i/ vowel sound.

- **Look and say. Complete the pattern.**

Mathematical Thinking

Learning to Know

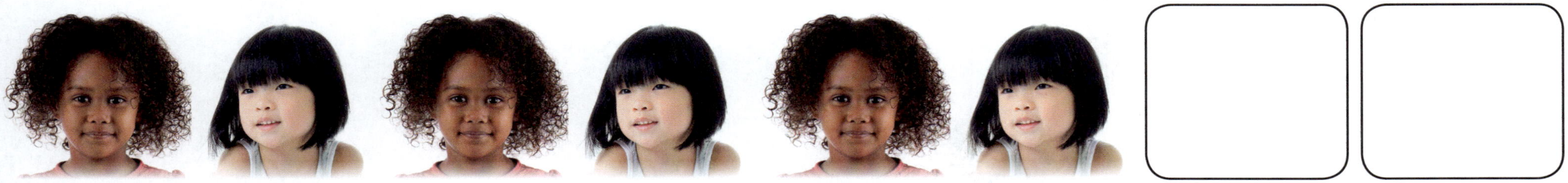

Objectives: Complete a simple pattern.

Unit 1

- **Listen. Circle what the children like about themselves.** 🎧 12 ✏️

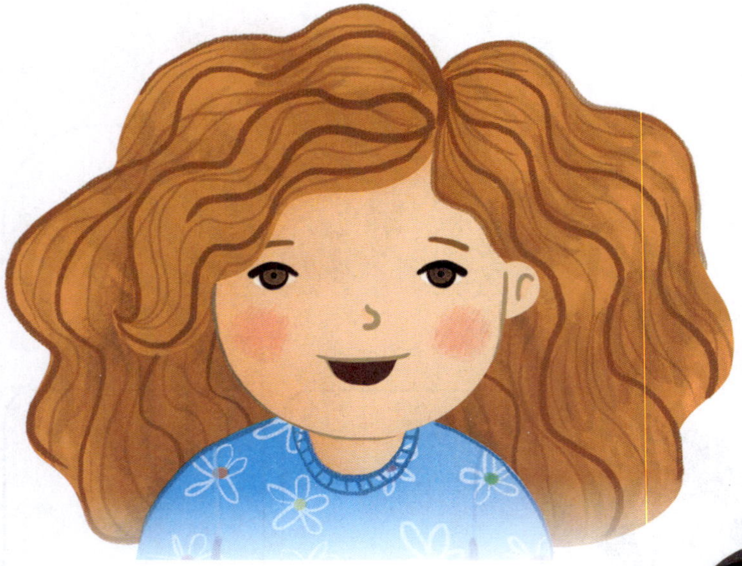

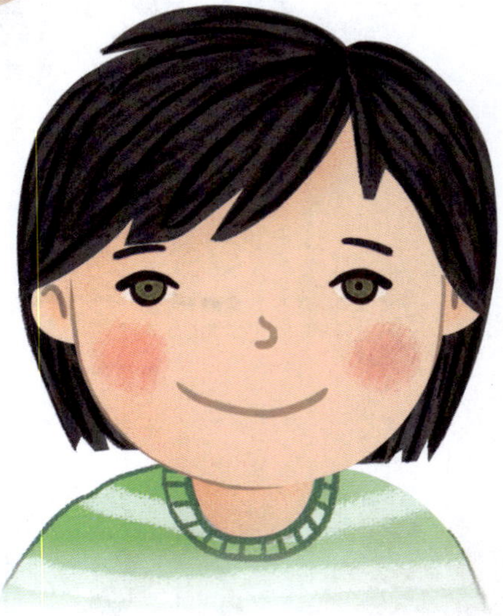

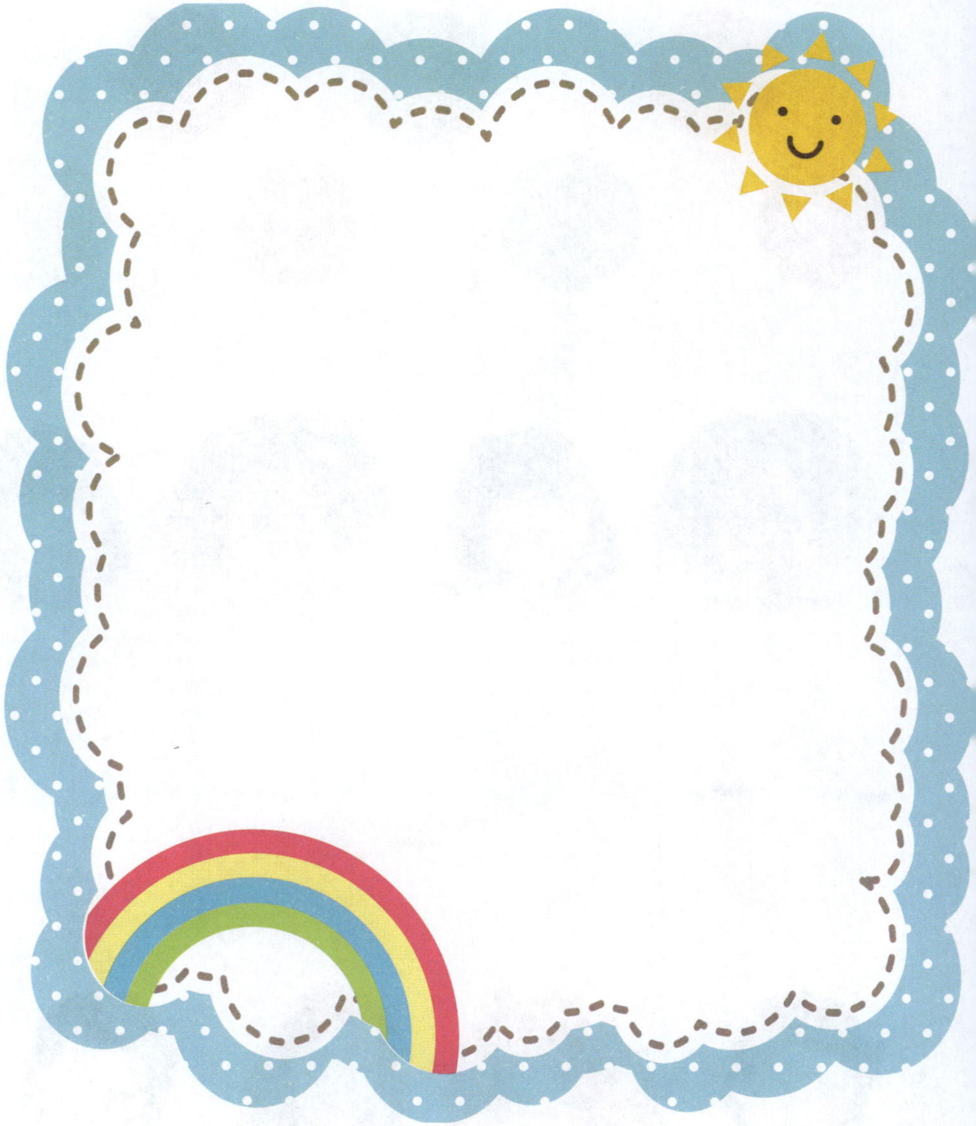

- **Draw what you like about yourself. Tell a friend.** ✏️ 👄

Objectives: Use target language to talk about what students like about themselves.

Listen and match.

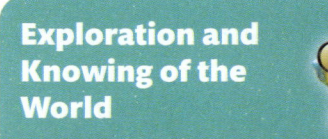
Exploration and Knowing of the World
Learning to Do

Think!
What kind of hair do you have in your family?

Objectives: Explore the idea that type of hair may vary in different parts of the world.

Unit 1

21

● **Listen and answer. Is the boy different? Why? Tell a friend.** 🎧 14 👄

Personal, Social, and Emotional Development

Learning to Live Together
Learning to Live with Others

22 Unit 1

Objectives: Understand that everybody looks different and that it is important to be kind to each other.

Listen and say what the problem is.

Literacy
Learning to Know

Think!
Is it day or night when you put on your pajamas?

Objectives: Listen to, understand, and retell a story about daily routines.

Unit 1

● **Listen. Match the pictures to their sound. Trace.**

Phonemic Awareness
Learning to Know

o   u

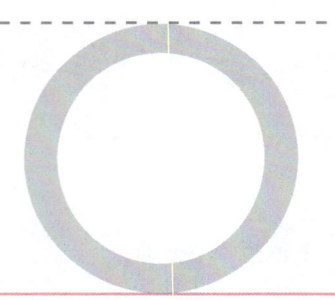

Unit 1

Objectives: Identify words with the short /o/ and /u/ vowel sounds.

Count. Color. Write.

Mathematical Thinking
Learning to Know

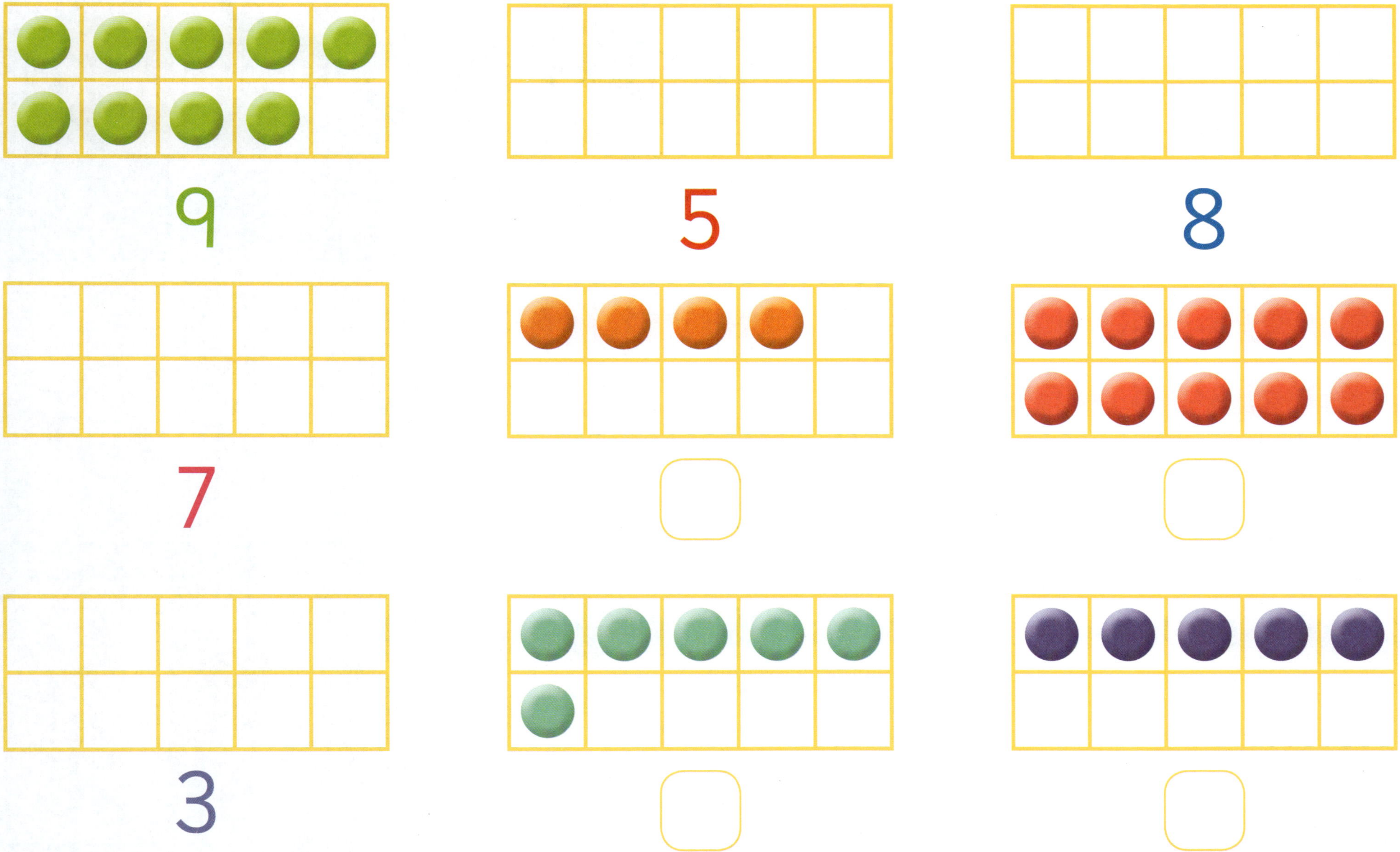

9

5

8

7

3

Objectives: Match numbers and objects.

Unit 1

● Listen, cut out, and paste what you use for each action. Say. 🎧 17 ✂️ 🍐 👄

Language Instruction and Communication
💡 Learning to Know

Objectives: Use target language to talk about daily routines.

- **Listen. Draw a dirty hand and a clean hand.**

Exploration and Knowing of the World

Learning to Do

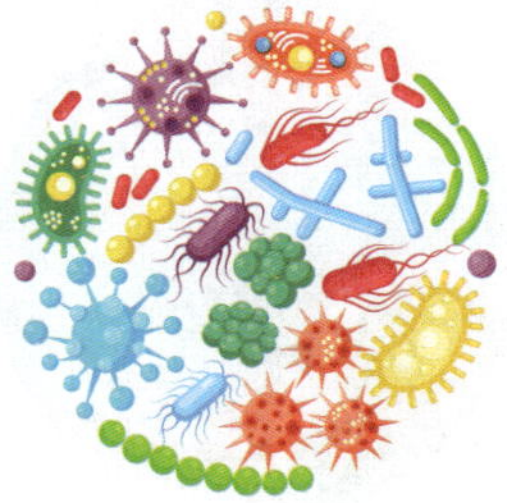

Think!
When do you wash your hands?

Objectives: Learn about how to keep your hands clean and prevent germs from spreading.

Unit 1

● **Listen and number the pictures. Which picture is correct?** 🎧 19 ✏️

Personal, Social, and Emotional Development

♥ Learning to Live Together
Learning to Live with Others

Think!
What do you do when you sneeze?

28 Unit 1

Objectives: Raise awareness of importance of good habits when sneezing.

Unit 2 Why do we go to school?

- Say what you like about school.

Listen and say. What do you do at school?

Literacy
Learning to Know

- Welcome to school!
- I play at school!
- I read at school!
- We learn at school!
- We have friends at school!

Unit 2

Objectives: Listen to and understand a story. Trace.

Listen and say. Circle the pictures with a long *a* sound.

Phonemic Awareness

Learning to Know

Objectives: Identify the long /a/ vowel sound.

Unit 2

Say, trace, and write.

Mathematical Thinking
Learning to Know

1	2	3	4	5
6	7	8	9	10
11		13	14	15
16		18		20
21	22	23	24	
26	27		29	30

32 unit 2

Objectives: Count to 30. Trace numbers and write missing numbers.

- **Look and circle things you do at school.**

Think!
What days do you go to school?

Objectives: Use target language to talk about the things we do at school.

Unit 2

● **Look, do, and think.**

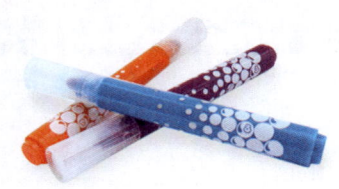

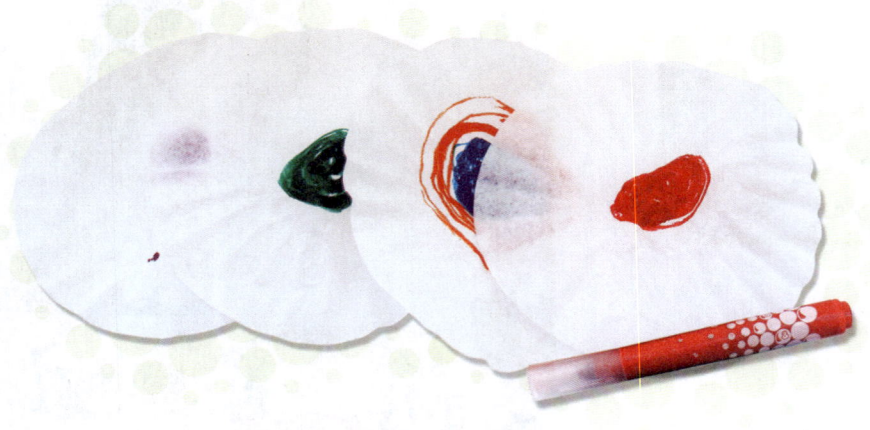

Think!
Is the filter absorbing the water?

Objectives: Do a science experiment in class.

- **Listen and look at the pictures. Draw the solution.**

Personal, Social, and Emotional Development

Learning to Live Together
Learning to Live with Others

Objectives: Learn why it is important to listen to the teacher and follow instructions.

Unit 2

● **Listen and circle.**

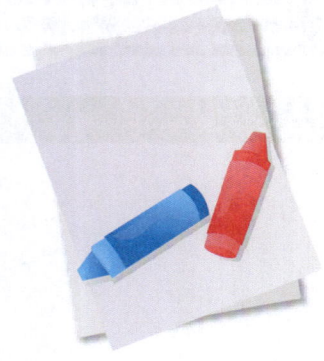

36 Unit 2

Objectives: Listen to a poem about school activities and answer questions.

● **Listen and say. Circle the pictures with a long e sound.** 🎧25 👄 ✏️

Phonemic Awareness

Learning to Know

e

Unit 2   37

Objectives: Identify the long /e/ vowel sound.

- **Extend the pattern. Draw.**

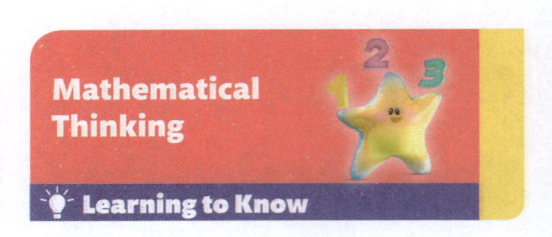

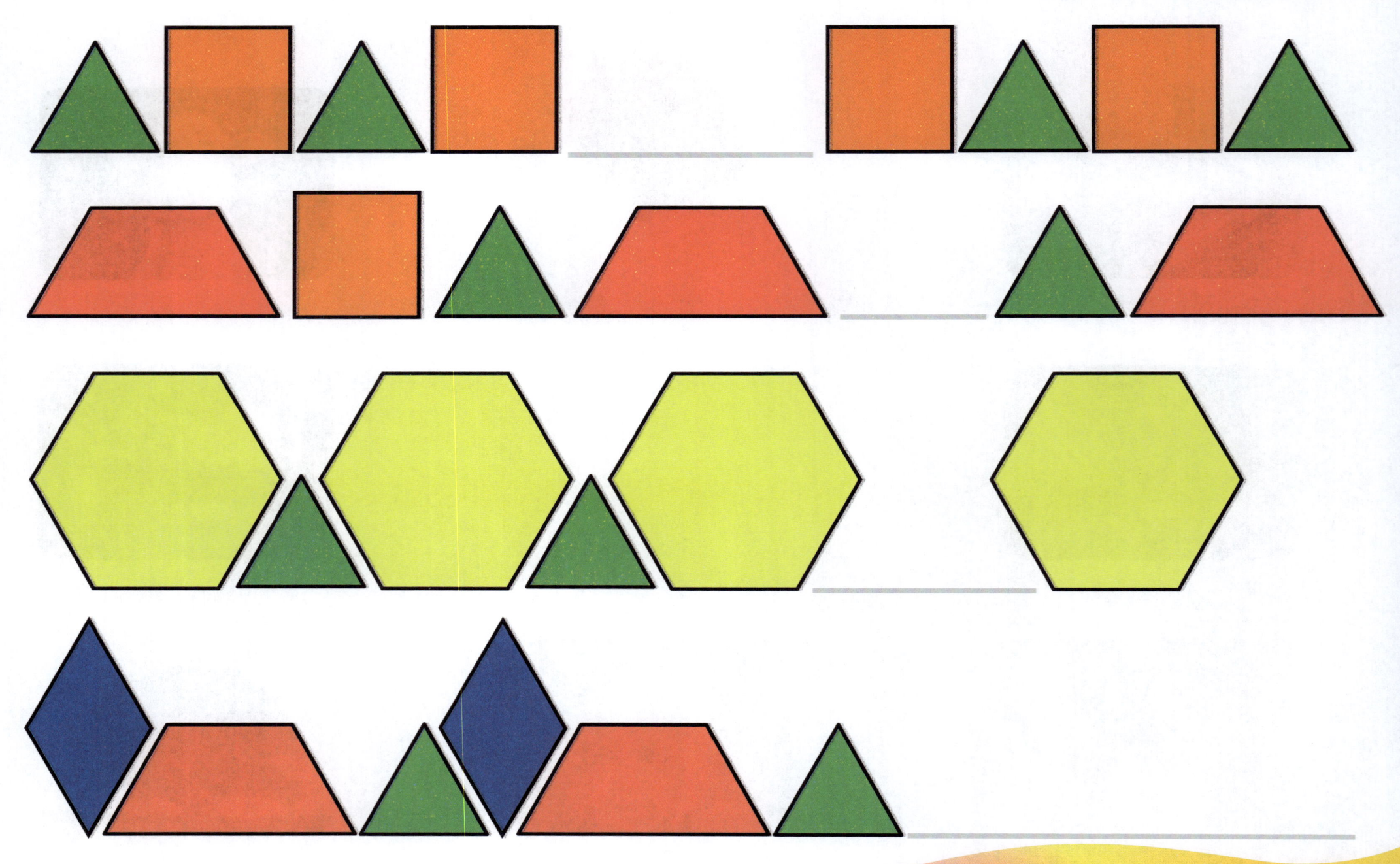

Mathematical Thinking
Learning to Know

38 Unit 2

Objectives: Name shapes and extend a complex pattern.

Listen and circle what you need. 🎧 ✏️

Language Instruction and Communication

💡 Learning to Know

Objectives: Use target language to talk about objects we use at school.

Unit 2

39

Make a butterfly mobile.

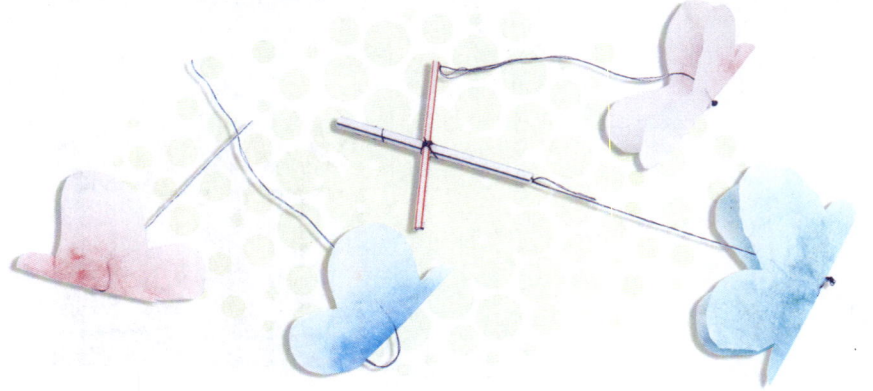

Exploration and Knowing of the World

Learning to Do

Think!
What is your favorite color?

40 Unit 2

Objectives: Recall the science experiment from the previous week and record the results.

- **Listen. Check the right way. Cross out the wrong way.** 🎧 27 ✓ ✗

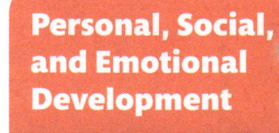

Personal, Social, and Emotional Development

Learning to Live Together
Learning to Live with Others

Think!
How do you feel when your classroom is messy?

Objectives: Learn to take care of classroom items and why it's important to use them carefully (e.g. scissors).

Unit 2

● **Listen and match.** 🎧 28

Literacy

💡 Learning to Know

42　Unit 2

Objectives: Listen to, understand, and sing a song about why school is important.

● **Listen, point, and say. Connect the pictures with a long *i* sound.** 🎧29 👄 🔗

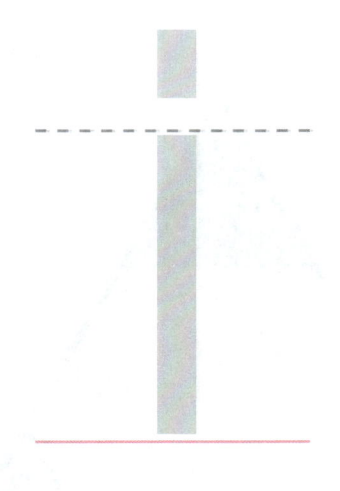

Phonemic Awareness
💡 Learning to Know

Objectives: Identify the long /i/ vowel sound.

Unit 2

43

- **Use pattern blocks.**

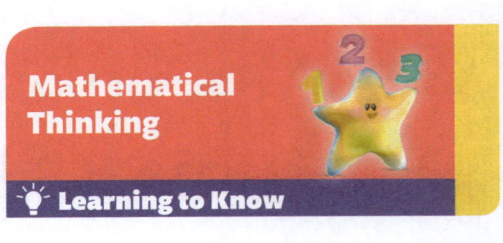

Mathematical Thinking
Learning to Know

Objectives: Put together shapes to make a different shape.

- **Listen and cross out. Who is not following the rules?** 🎧30 ❌

- **Play *Starfish Says*.**

Objectives: Use target language to talk about classroom rules.

Unit 2

45

● **Listen and make a bar chart.** 🎧 ✏️

5
4
3
2
1

Exploration and Knowing of the World

Learning to Do

Think!
How many animals do you have at home?

46　Unit 2

Objectives: Learn to make a simple bar chart.

- **Listen and number.**

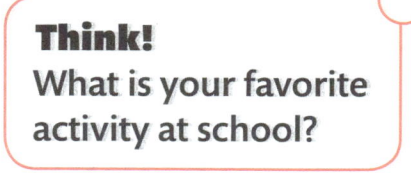

Personal, Social, and Emotional Development

Learning to Live Together
Learning to Live with Others

Think!
What is your favorite activity at school?

Objectives: Remember and follow instructions.

Unit 2

47

- **Listen and think. What are the children playing?** 🎧 💡

Literacy

💡 **Learning to Know**

- **Play *The Opposite Game*.** 🏐

48 Unit 2

Objectives: Listen to, understand, and retell a story about school activities and listening to the teacher.

- **Listen and say. Match the pictures to their sound.**

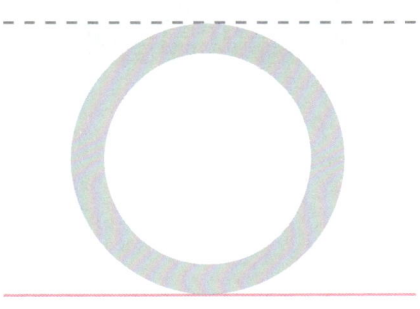

o

u

Unit 2

49

Objectives: Identify long /o/ and /u/ vowel sounds.

Phonemic Awareness

Learning to Know

Look at the class calendar. Listen and write.

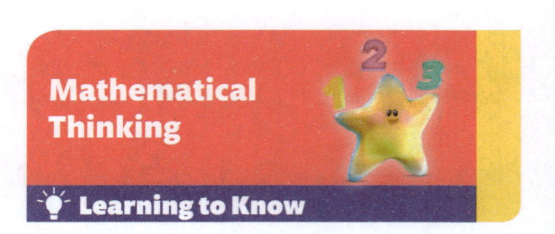

Month: _____

Sunday	Monday	Tuesday	Wednesday	Thursday	Friday	Saturday

Mathematical Thinking
Learning to Know

Objectives: Write missing numbers. Say the day and date.

Listen and check the correct behavior. 🎧 35 ✅

Language Instruction and Communication

💡 Learning to Know

Objectives: Use target language to talk about sharing and being kind to others in the classroom.

Unit 2

Listen and color. Which school is similar to yours? 🎧 36 ✏️

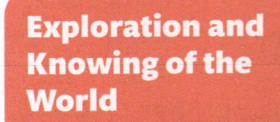

Exploration and Knowing of the World

✋ Learning to Do

52 Unit 2

Objectives: Find out about different types of classrooms and schools around the world and compare with own experiences.

Cut out and paste.

Personal, Social, and Emotional Development

Learning to Live Together
Learning to Live with Others

Think!
What makes you happy at school?

Objectives: Learn why we need to be kind to others at school.

Unit 2

53

Unit 3 How can you help your family at home?

- **Circle family members.**

- **Listen. What does the boy need to help? Match.**

Literacy

Learning to Know

Think!
What chores do you and your family members do at home?

Objectives: Listen to a dialogue and answer questions about helping family members at home.

Unit 3

55

- **Listen. Circle the pictures that begin with an *m* sound.**

Phonemic Awareness

Learning to Know

m

56　Unit 3

Objectives: Identify the initial /m/ sound.

- **Say, trace, and write.**

1	2	3	4	5	6	7	8	9	10
11		13	14	15	16	17		19	
21		23		25	26	27	28	29	30
31	32	33		35	36	37		39	40
41		43	44	45	46	47		49	50

Mathematical Thinking

Learning to Know

Objectives: Count to 50. Identify, trace, and write missing numbers.

Unit 3

● **Listen. What are they hiding? Circle.**

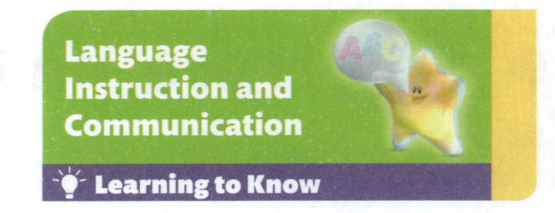

Unit 3

Objectives: Use target language (new and revised) to talk about family members.

- **Circle the young people green 🟢 and the old people red 🔴.** ✏️

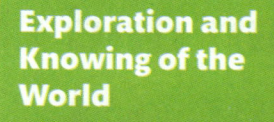

Exploration and Knowing of the World

Learning to Do

Think!
Who is old in your family?

Objectives: Learn to tell the difference between older and younger members of the family.

Unit 3

59

- **Listen and circle the child who is four.** 🎧 ✏️

Personal, Social, and Emotional Development

Learning to Live Together
Learning to Live with Others

Think!
How old are you?

- **Find out about a friend's age.**

60 Unit 3

Objectives: Talk about students' age.

● **Listen and match.** 🎧 42

Literacy

Learning to Know

Think!
What do you do to help at home?

Objectives: Listen to a poem about helping extended family members and answering questions.

Unit 3

61

● **Listen. Color the pictures of words that begin with s.**

Phonemic Awareness
Learning to Know

S

Objectives: Identify the initial /s/ sound.

Unit 3

62

Extend the pattern. Paste.

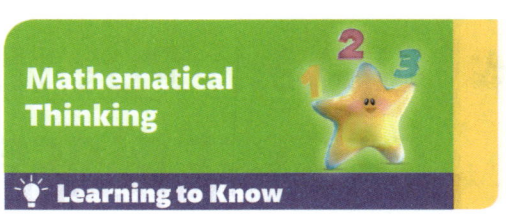

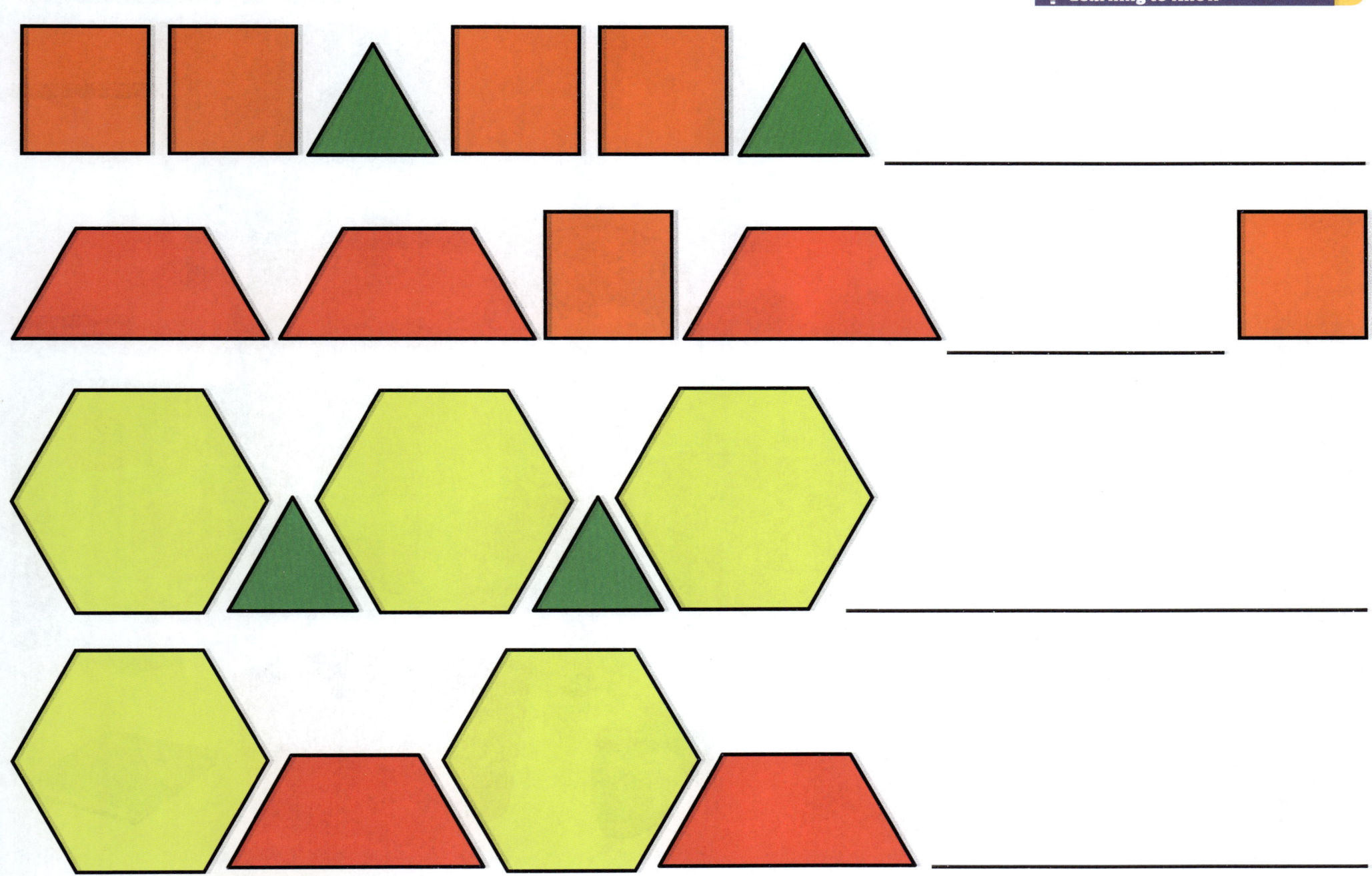

Mathematical Thinking

Learning to Know

Objectives: Name shapes and extend a complex pattern.

Unit 3

- **Listen. Put the objects in the correct place.** 🎧 44

● **Look. Cut and paste.**

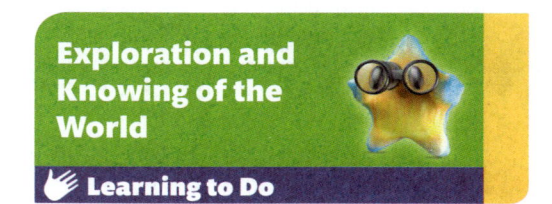

Exploration and Knowing of the World
Learning to Do

Think!
Do you look like someone in your family?

Objectives: Talk about similarities between older members of the family and own features.

Unit 3

65

- **Listen and number the pictures.**

Unit 3

Objectives: Learn about why it is important to help keep your home clean.

Listen. Draw the missing objects. Circle what you do at home.

Literacy

Learning to Know

Objectives: Listen to, understand, and sing a song about helping out at home.

Unit 3

67

● **Listen. Match the pictures to their initial sound. Trace.**

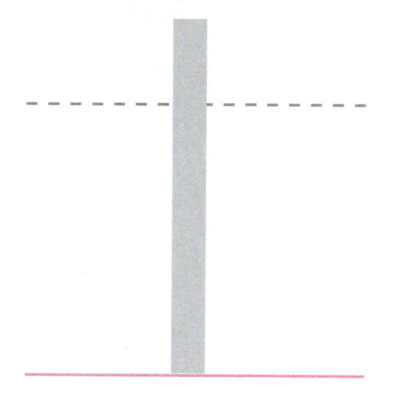

Phonemic Awareness
Learning to Know

d

l

Unit 3

Objectives: Identify the initial /d/ and /l/ sounds.

Draw the people. Say.

Mathematical Thinking
Learning to Know

parents

brothers, sisters, and me

grandparents

Objectives: Make a simple pictograph.

Unit 3

69

- **Listen. Circle where to find what Susy wants.** 🎧 48 ✏️

- **Say the objects and where they are.** 👄

70 Unit 3

Objectives: Use target language to talk about rooms in the house, household objects, and where they are located.

- **Circle the small animals. Color their homes.**

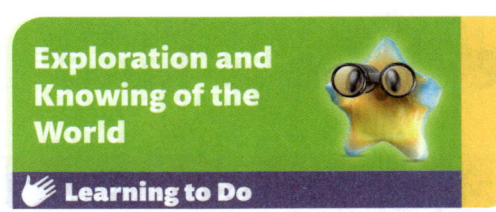

Exploration and Knowing of the World

Learning to Do

Think!
Say where other animals live.

Objectives: Know where animals live.

Unit 3

71

- **Who is kind? Circle.**

Personal, Social, and Emotional Development

Learning to Live Together
Learning to Live with Others

Think!
How do you help at home?

72   Unit 3

Objectives: Learn about being kind to older members of the family (e.g. grandparents).

- **Who does Debbie help? Listen and circle.**

Literacy
Learning to Know

Objectives: Listen to, understand, and retell a story about families helping each other at home.

Unit 3

73

- **Listen. Circle the pictures with a *t* sound. Trace.**

Phonemic Awareness
Learning to Know

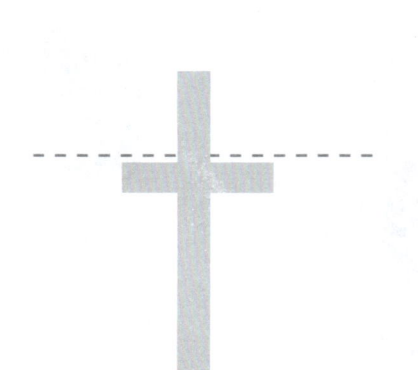

74 Unit 3

Objectives: Identify the initial /t/ sound.

- **Work in pairs. Draw objects that are longer, the same, or shorter than your yarn.**

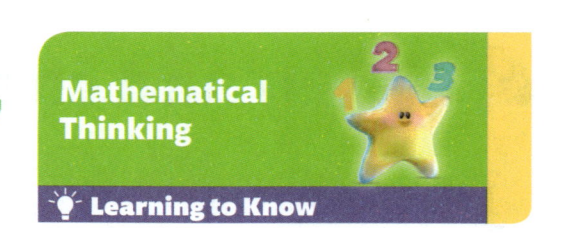

My yarn _____

Shorter	Same	Longer

Objectives: Measure objects using non-standard units.

Listen and check the safe actions. 🎧 51 ✓

Language Instruction and Communication

💡 Learning to Know

Unit 3

Objectives: Use target language to talk about safety at home.

Listen. Cross out the dangerous situations. 🎧 52 ✗

Exploration and Knowing of the World
Learning to Do

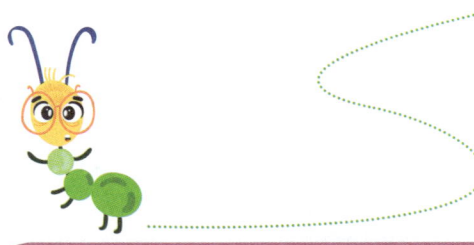

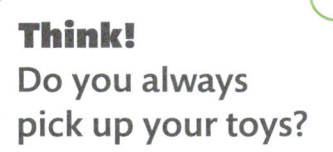

Think!
Do you always pick up your toys?

Objectives: Learn about safety at home and following instructions.

Unit 3

77

Listen. Color the safe option.

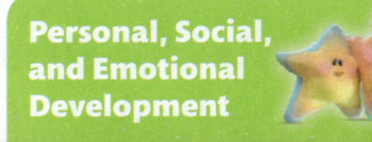

Personal, Social, and Emotional Development

Learning to Live Together
Learning to Live with Others

Think! Do you ask for help?

Objectives: Learn about safety at home and asking for help with certain chores to stay safe.

Unit 3

78

Unit 4 Why do you feel hot or cold?

- **Listen and say.** 🎧 55 👄

79

Listen and color.

Literacy

Learning to Know

Objectives: Listen to a dialogue about different types of weather and answer questions.

Unit 4

● **Listen. Color the pictures that begin with p.**

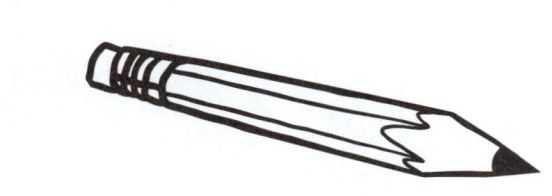

Phonemic Awareness
Learning to Know

Objectives: Identify and say words with the initial /p/ sound.

Unit 4

Point and say. Trace and write.

| 1 | 2 | 3 | 4 | 5 | 6 | 7 | 8 | 9 | 10 |

| 11 | | 13 | | 15 | | 17 | | 19 | |

| 21 | | 23 | | 25 | | 27 | | 29 | 30 |

Mathematical Thinking — Learning to Know

Objectives: Skip-count by 2's to 30. Trace numbers.

- **Listen and number.**

Language Instruction and Communication

💡 Learning to Know

Objectives: Use target language to talk about the weather.

Unit 4

83

Explore and match.

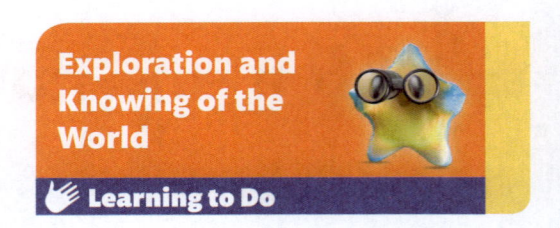

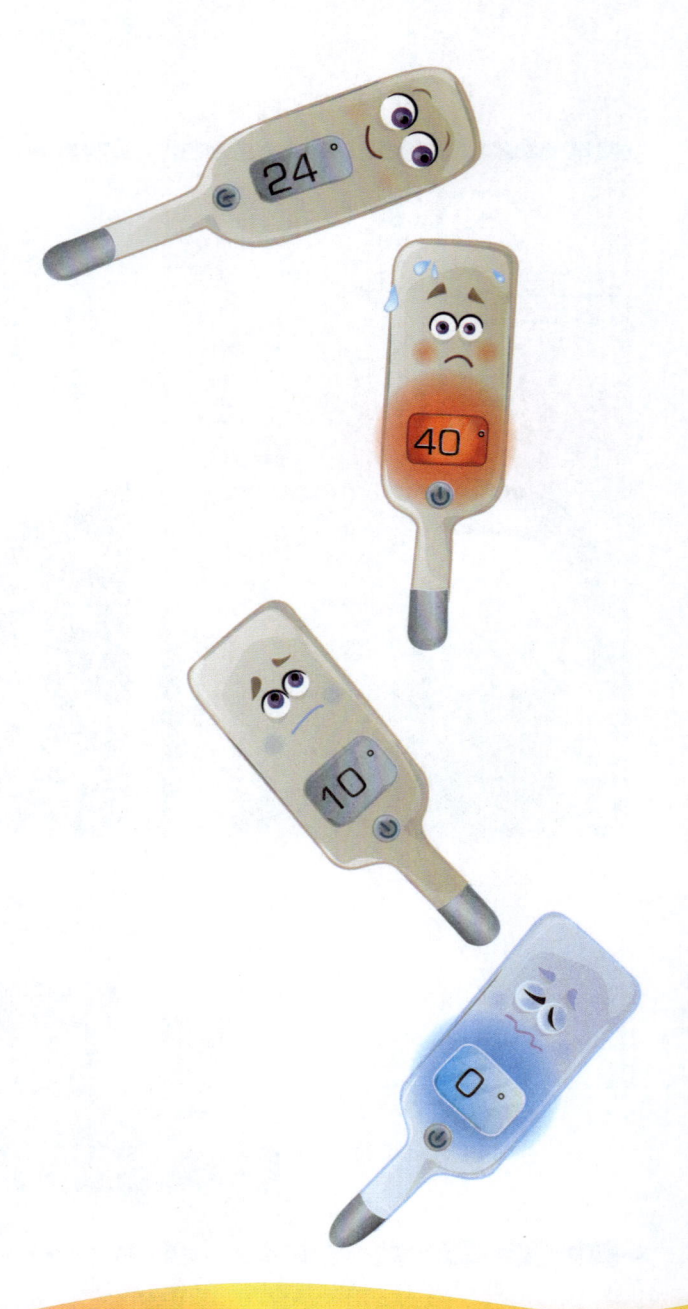

Exploration and Knowing of the World

Learning to Do

84 Unit 4

Objectives: Learn about temperature, how we feel when it is hot or cold, and how to record the temperature.

● Listen. Look and circle. 🎧 59 👁 ✏️

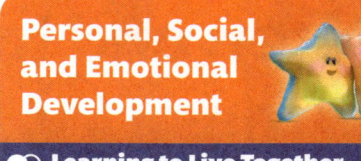

Personal, Social, and Emotional Development

♥ Learning to Live Together
Learning to Live with Others

Think!
How can you help people that do not have clothes for cold or rainy weather?

Objectives: Learn why it is important to dress appropriately for the weather.

Unit 4

85

● **Listen and look. Draw appropriate clothes.**

Literacy
Learning to Know

Think!
Are you cold today?

Unit 4

Objectives: Listen to, understand, and retell a poem about different temperatures.

- **Listen. Circle the pictures that begin with *p*. Trace.** 🎧61 ✏️

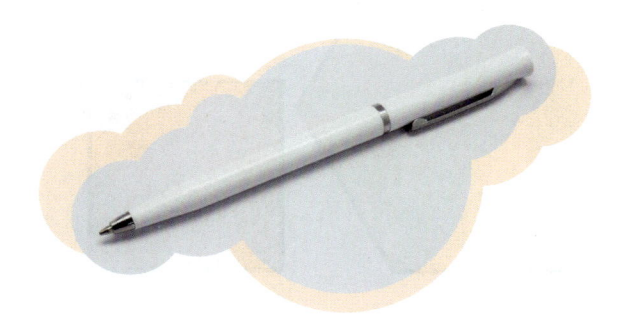

p

Phonemic Awareness
Learning to Know

Objectives: Identify and say words with the initial /p/ sound.

Unit 4

87

- **Extend the pattern. Paste.**

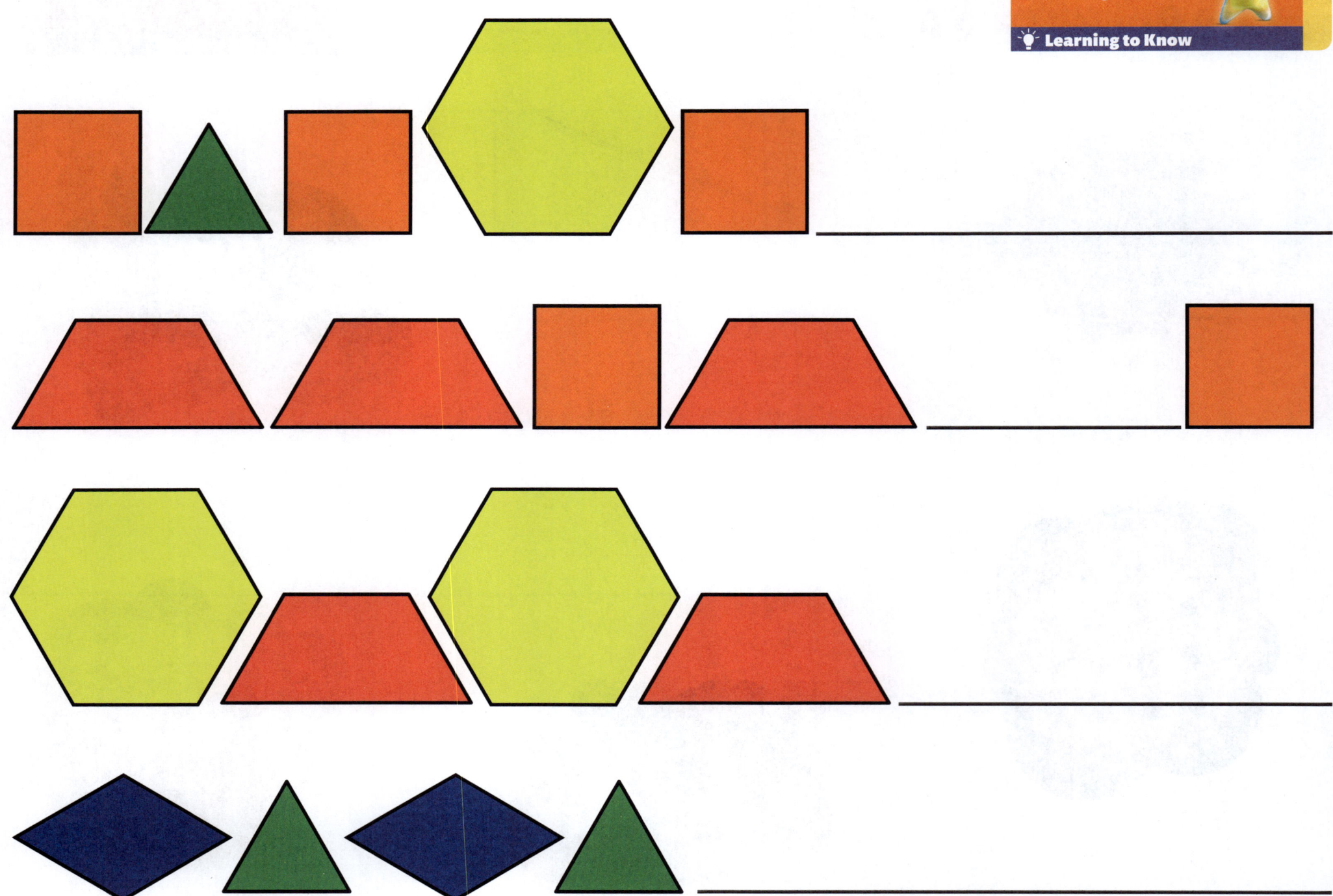

Listen and number.

Objectives: Use target language to talk about the temperature and what we wear when it is hot, cold, cool, and warm.

Language Instruction and Communication

Learning to Know

Unit 4

89

- **Listen and color. What do you have to wear when it is sunny?**

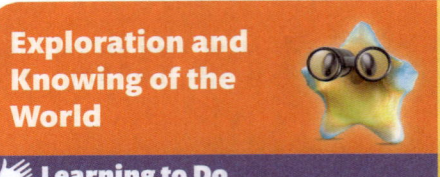

Exploration and Knowing of the World

Learning to Do

Think!
Why is it important to wear a hat when it is sunny?

90 Unit 4

Objectives: Learn about how children protect their bodies when it is hot.

Look and match. What does she need to keep warm?

Objectives: Learn how to keep warm when it is cold.

Personal, Social, and Emotional Development

Learning to Live Together
Learning to Live with Others

Unit 4

91

Listen. Cut and paste. 🎧 64

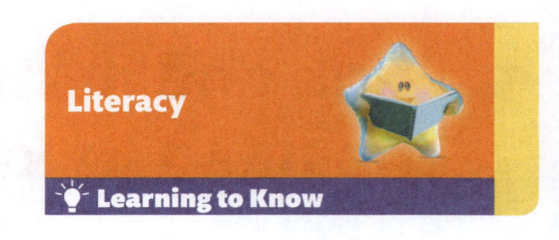

Literacy

💡 Learning to Know

Think!
Is it hot outside today?

92 Unit 4

Objectives: Listen to, understand, and sing a song about the clothes we wear in different weather.

Listen. Connect the pictures that begin with *c* to the cage. Trace.

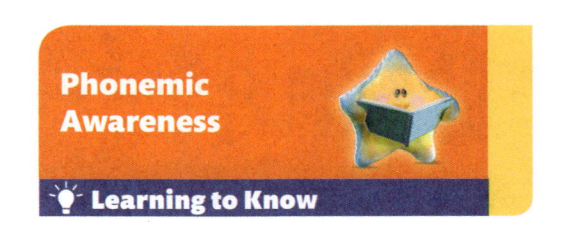

Phonemic Awareness
Learning to Know

Objectives: Identify and say words with the initial /c/ sound.

Unit 4

93

● **Make a hexagon. Paste.**

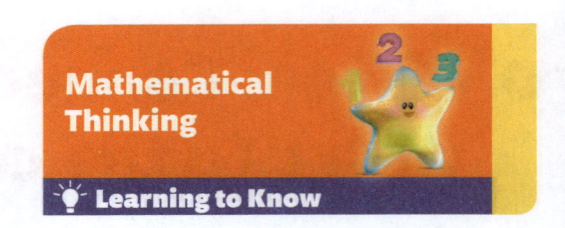

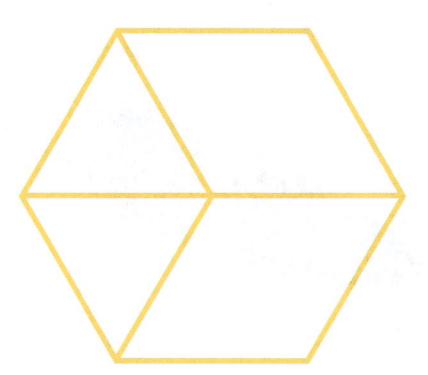

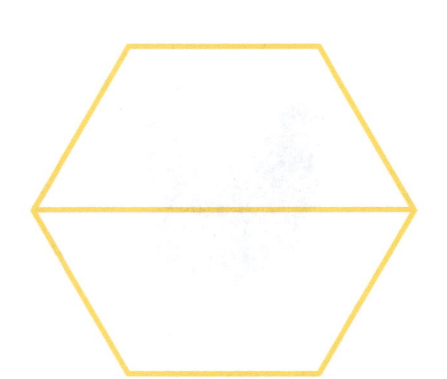

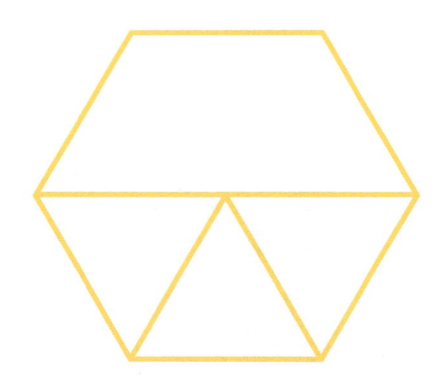

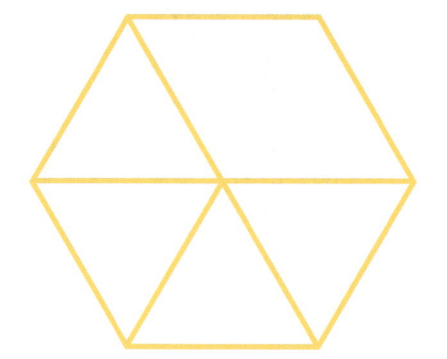

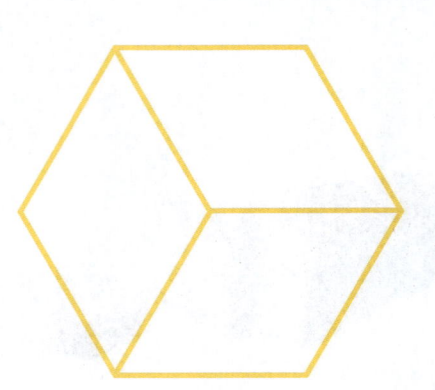

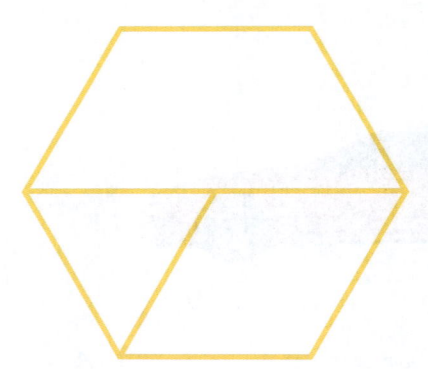

Mathematical Thinking

Learning to Know

94 Unit 4

Objectives: Know that different shapes can be used to make other shapes.

- Listen and number. 🎧 ✏️

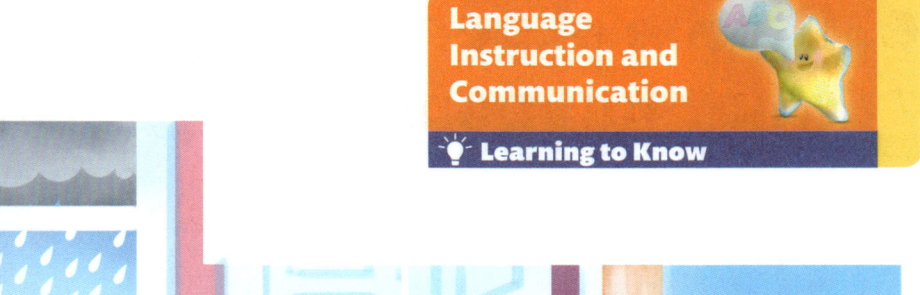

Language Instruction and Communication
💡 Learning to Know

- What do you wear when it is raining? Cold? Tell a friend. 👄

Objectives: Use target language to talk about the clothes we wear in different types of weather.

Unit 4

95

- **Do the experiment. Listen and draw what happens.** 🎧 ✏️

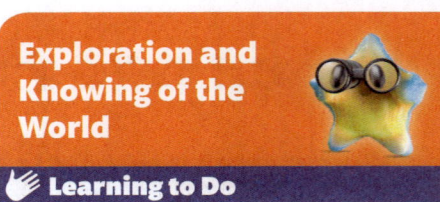

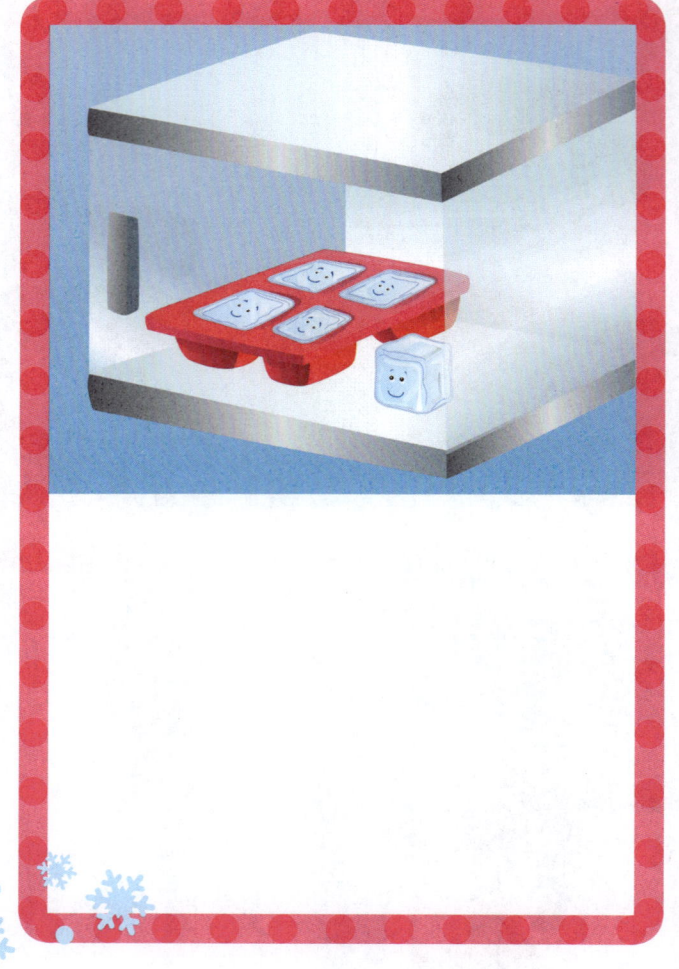

Exploration and Knowing of the World

Learning to Do

Think!
What color is ice?

Objectives: Do an experiment and record the results.

96 Unit 4

- **Do the experiment. Is the sun strong today? How do you know?**

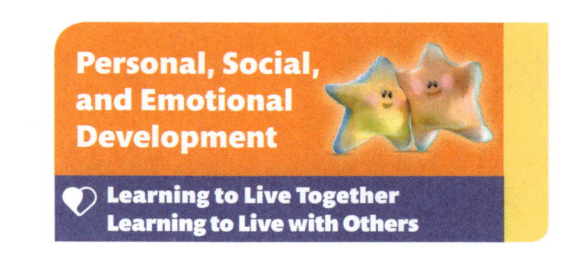

Personal, Social, and Emotional Development
Learning to Live Together
Learning to Live with Others

- **How do you protect yourself from the sun? Tell a friend.**

Objectives: Learn why it is important to protect ourselves from the sun.

Unit 4

● **Listen. Check how the girl protects herself from the sun.** 🎧 ✓

Literacy
💡 Learning to Know

98 Unit 4

Objectives: Listen to, understand, and retell a story about how to protect ourselves in different types of weather.

Listen. Circle the pictures that begin with *n*. Trace.

n

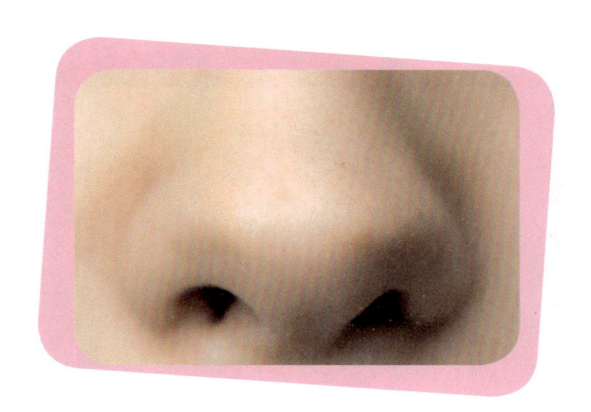

Objectives: Identify and say words with the initial /n/ sound.

Phonemic Awareness

Learning to Know

Unit 4

● **Color the heavier object.**

Mathematical Thinking
Learning to Know

100 Unit 4

Objectives: Think about mass.

Look and color who is staying safe from the sun.

Language Instruction and Communication
- Learning to Know

Think!
How do you stay safe in the sun?

Objectives: Use target language to talk about what we can do to stay safe in the sun.

Unit 4

- **Color the winter clothes blue and the summer clothes red.**

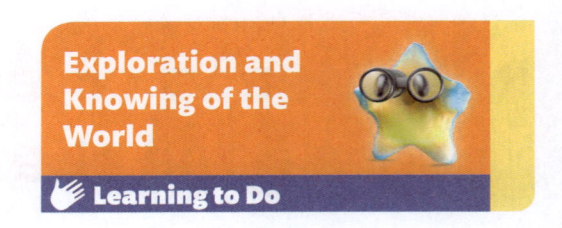

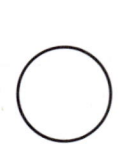

Exploration and Knowing of the World — Learning to Do

- **Listen and say. Which of the clothes is thick? Which is thin?**

Unit 4

Objectives: Identify summer and winter clothes according to how thick or thin they are.

● **Listen and follow. Draw a happy or a sad face.** 🎧71 ✏️

Personal, Social, and Emotional Development

Learning to Live Together
Learning to Live with Others

Think!
When do you feel happy...
on a sunny day or on a cold day?

Objectives: Talk about how you feel when it is hot and cold.

Unit 4

103

- **Listen and sing. Trace.**

- **Say what the children see in the sky.**

104 Unit 4

Objectives: Listen to, understand, and retell a poem about to things we see in the sky.

- **Draw a picture that begins with *p* and a picture that begins with *c*. Tell a friend.**

Phonemic Awareness

Learning to Know

Objectives: Identify and say words with the initial /p/ and /c/ sounds.

Unit 4

- **Color the squares.**

Mathematical Thinking

Learning to Know

106 Unit 4

Objectives: Make a simple bar graph.

- **Listen and number the pictures.**

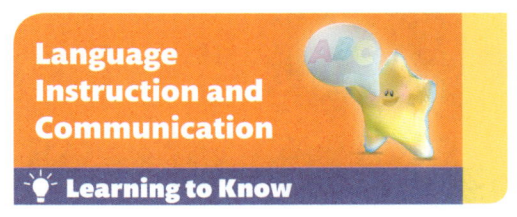

Language Instruction and Communication
Learning to Know

Objectives: Use target language to talk about things we see in the sky during the day and at night.

Unit 4

107

- **Draw the things you see.**

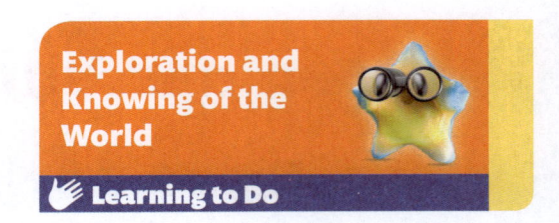

Exploration and Knowing of the World
Learning to Do

| Day | Day/Night | Night |

Think!
What do you see in the sky today?

Unit 4

Objectives: Record things we see in the sky during the day and at night.

● **Match.**

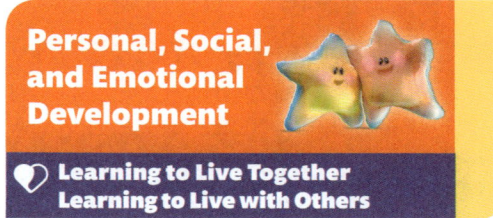

day

night

● **Say what you do in the day and what you do at night.**

Personal, Social, and Emotional Development
Learning to Live Together
Learning to Live with Others

Think!
What do you do every morning?

Objectives: Classify activities we do during the day and at night.

Unit 4

● **Listen and number the pictures.**

● **Why is the boy happy in the snow and not happy in the sun?**

110 Unit 4

Objectives: Listen to, understand, and retell a story about natural phenomena.

- **Match the pictures to their sound. Say.**

Phonemic Awareness
Learning to Know

n
c
p

Objectives: Identify and say words with the initial /p/, /c/, and /n/ sounds.

Unit 4

Count. Color. Write.

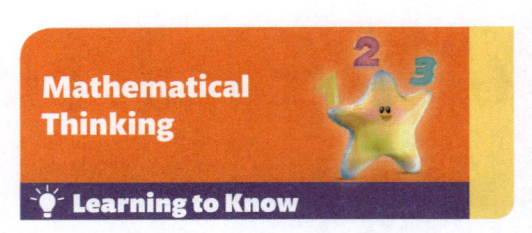

0 1 2 3 4 5 6 7 8 9 10 11 12 13 14 15 16 17 18 19 20

16

Draw.

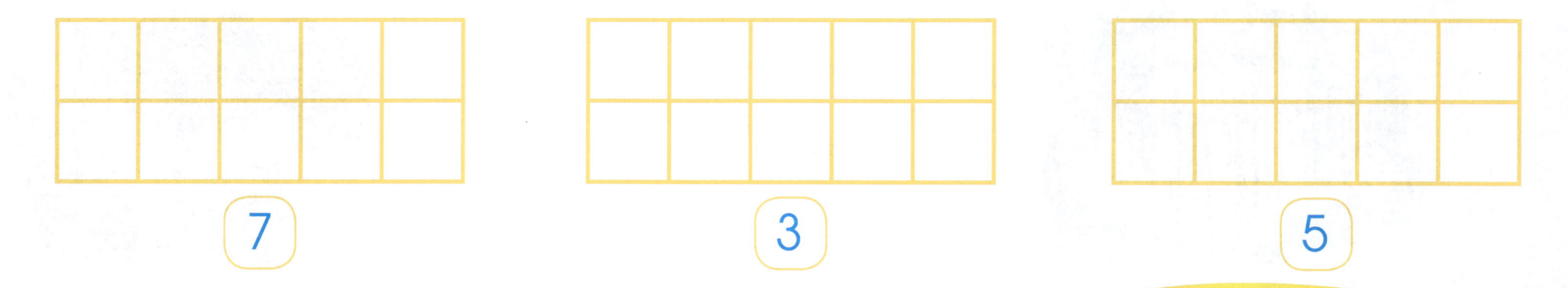

7   3   5

Objectives: Count up to 20.

- **Check what your friends like or don't like.** ✓ ✗

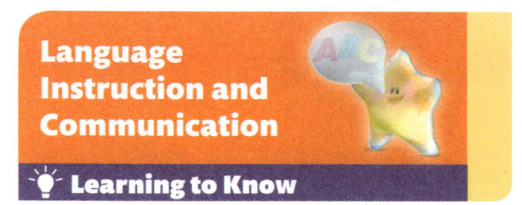

Language Instruction and Communication
Learning to Know

- **Count your results and share with the class.**

Objectives: Use target language to talk about natural phenomena.

Unit 4

● **Listen and trace.** 🎧 ✏️

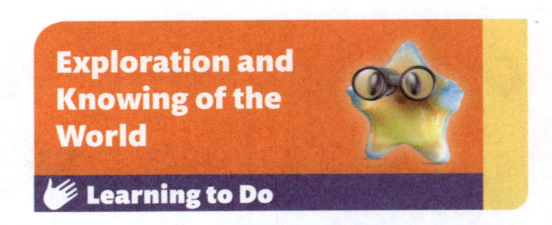

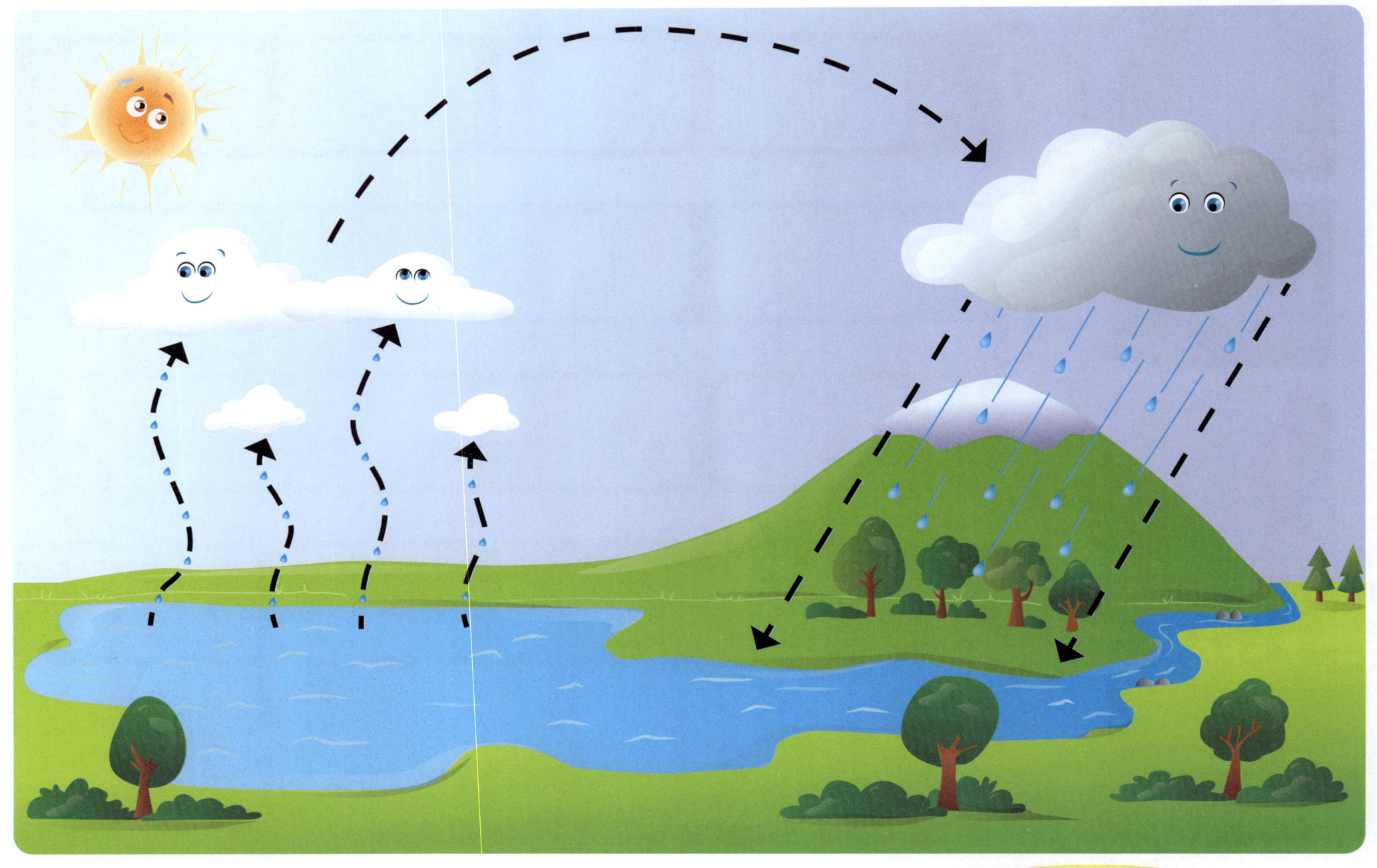

Exploration and Knowing of the World

Learning to Do

114　Unit 4

Objectives: Learn about the water cycle.

- **Make a collage of what you like about rainy days.**

Personal, Social, and Emotional Development

Learning to Live Together
Learning to Live with Others

Objectives: Talk about the type of weather they like.

Unit 4

Unit 5 What other living things are around us?

- Circle the bugs. Where can you see animals like these?

- **Listen and circle the bugs. Sing.** 🎧 ✏️ 👄

Literacy

Learning to Know

Objectives: Listen to a song about insects and answer questions about it.

Unit 5

- **Listen. Color pictures that begin with b.**

  Phonemic Awareness — Learning to Know

  b

- **Trace.**

Unit 5

Objectives: Identify and say words with the initial /b/ sound.

Point, say, trace, and write.

Mathematical Thinking — Learning to Know

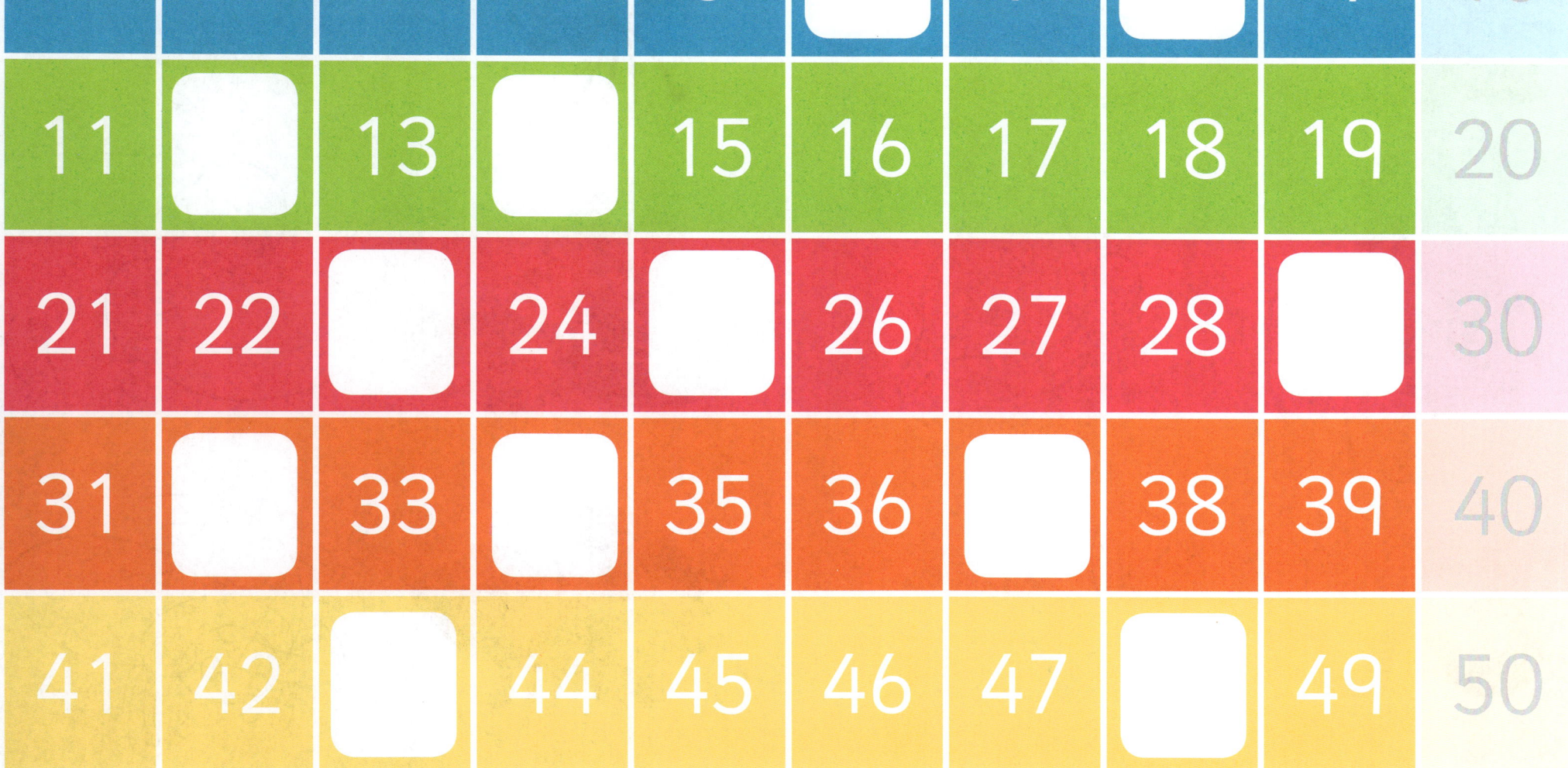

1	2	3	4	5		7		9	10
11		13		15	16	17	18	19	20
21	22		24		26	27	28		30
31		33		35	36		38	39	40
41	42		44	45	46	47		49	50

Objectives: Trace numbers. Write numbers. Count by 10's.

Unit 5

Listen and say the poem. Listen to the teacher and color. 🎧79 👄 ✏️

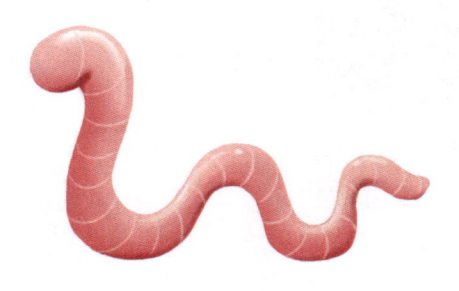

Language Instruction and Communication
Learning to Know

120 Unit 5

Objectives: Use target language to talk about insects.

- **Listen and look.**

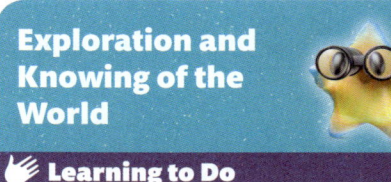

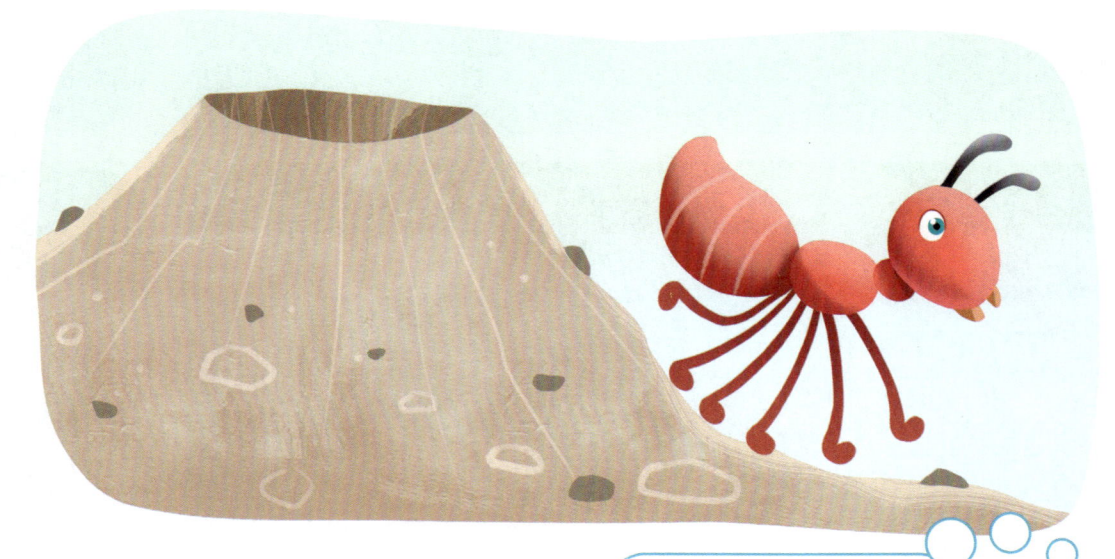

- **Circle the insect with six blue legs.**
  Circle the insect with two green wings.

Exploration and Knowing of the World
Learning to Do

Think! How many legs do spiders have?

Objectives: Learn about insects and their different characteristics.

Unit 5

121

Listen and trace. How are all living things connected? 🎧 ✏️

Personal, Social, and Emotional Development

Learning to Live Together
Learning to Live with Others

122 Unit 5

Objectives: Learn why insects are important, why we need to respect them, and how they are a part of food chains.

Listen and number. Act out.

Literacy

💡 Learning to Know

Think!
What do the insects do in the story?

Objectives: Listen to, understand, and narrate a story about insects and plants that live in the yard.

Unit 5

- **Listen. Color the pictures that begin with *f*. Trace.**

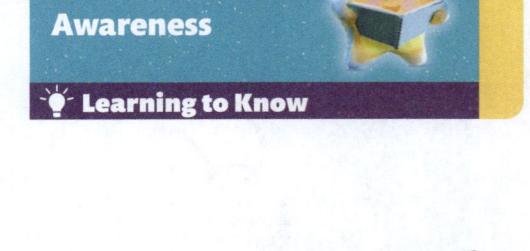

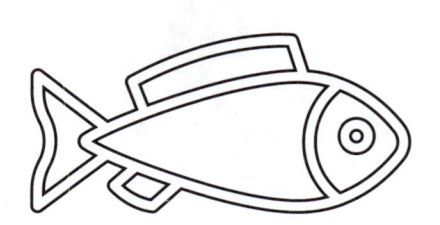

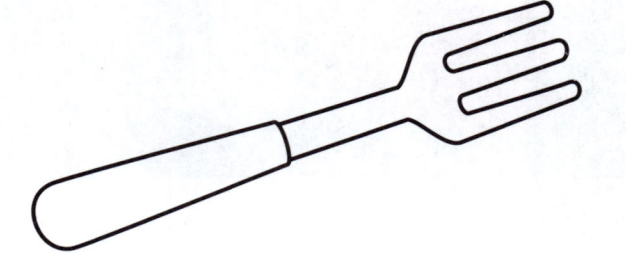

Phonemic Awareness

Learning to Know

f

124 Unit 5

Objectives: Identify and say words with the initial /f/ sound.

- **Draw 2 cats in the grass, 2 butterflies over the grass, and 2 worms under the grass.**

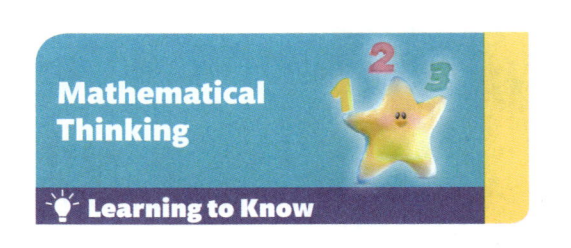

Mathematical Thinking
Learning to Know

butterfly

cat

worm

- **Tell a friend where the animals are.**

Objectives: Can identify *in*, *over*, and *under*.

- **Listen and follow. What do plants need to grow?**

- **Check what the boy gets in the story.** ✓

126 Unit 5

Objectives: Use target language to talk about plants.

Listen and circle the honey.

Exploration and Knowing of the World

Learning to Do

Think!
Do you like honey?

Objectives: Learn about bees and how they make honey.

Unit 5 — 127

Listen and trace to connect. 🎧 ✏️

Personal, Social, and Emotional Development

💗 Learning to Live Together
Learning to Live with Others

Think!
How do we take care of plants?

128   Unit 5

Objectives: Learn about why plants are good for the planet and why we need to take care of them.

- **Listen and follow.**

Literacy

Learning to Know

- **Circle what comes from a seed.**

Objectives: Listen to and understand a dialogue about taking care of plants.

Unit 5

- **Listen. What is it? Trace to find out.** 🎧 ✏️

Phonemic Awareness

Learning to Know

r

Objectives: Identify and say words with the initial /r/ sound.

Say, sort, and draw.

Plants	Animals

Mathematical Thinking

Learning to Know

Objectives: Sort animals and plants.

Unit 5

131

Listen and sing. Cut and paste.

132 Unit 5

Objectives: Use target language to talk about planting seeds and growing plants.

Language Instruction and Communication

Learning to Know

Listen and follow. Circle the caterpillar red and the butterfly blue.

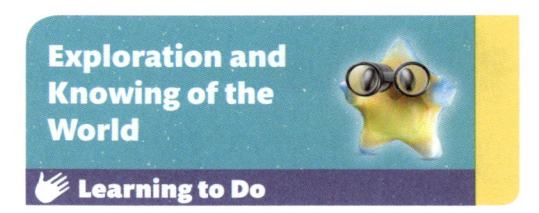

Exploration and Knowing of the World

Learning to Do

Think!
Do you like the caterpillar or the butterfly?

Objectives: Learn about the life cycle of a butterfly.

Unit 5

- **Listen and follow. Say what the children are doing.**

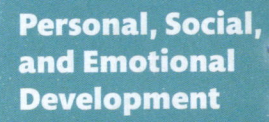

- **Draw a garden for your schoolyard.**

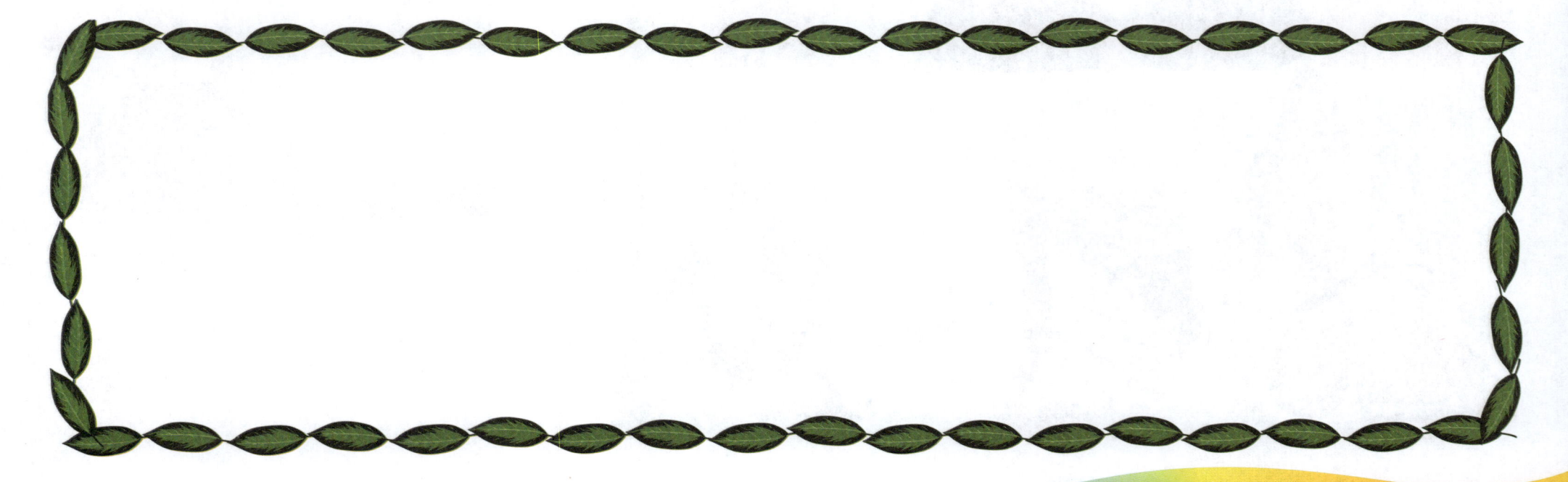

134 Unit 5

Objectives: Learn about schools in other countries that have their own yard for planting things.

- **Listen and circle the odd one out. Sing.**

- **Number the steps.**

Objectives: Listen to, understand, and sing a song about the elements that plants need to grow.

Unit 5

135

- **Color the *b* words green, the *f* words orange and the *r* words blue. Say.**

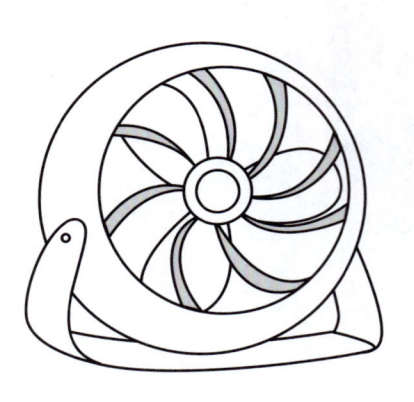

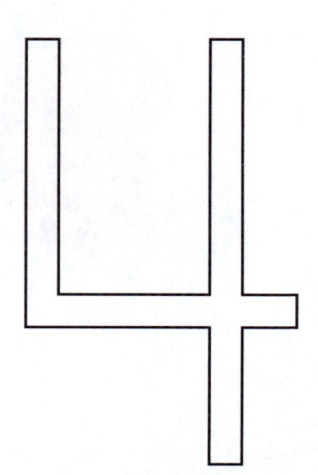

136 Unit 5

Objectives: Identify and say words with the initial /b/, /f/, and /r/ sounds.

Trace, match, and color.

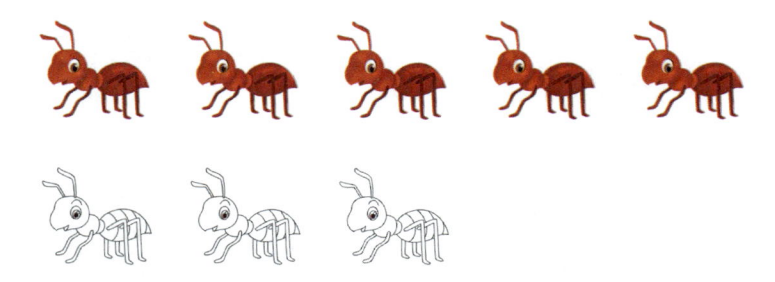

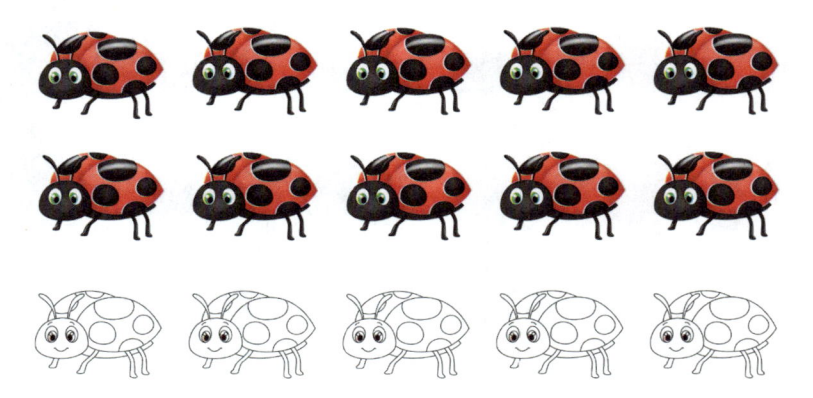

Mathematical Thinking
Learning to Know

7

13

4

15

8

Objectives: Match number of objects with numbers.

Unit 5 — 137

Listen and number.

Language Instruction and Communication

Learning to Know

Unit 5

Objectives: Use target language to talk about where insects live.

- **Look and match.**

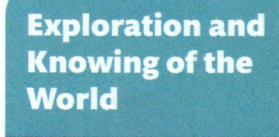

- **Do an experiment. Follow your teacher's instructions. Draw the results.**

Exploration and Knowing of the World

Learning to Do

Objectives: Learn about planting seeds and how to help them grow. Record results.

Unit 5

139

● **How do the insects make you feel? Color.**

Personal, Social, and Emotional Development

Learning to Live Together
Learning to Live with Others

Think!
How can we take care of insects?

140 Unit 5

Objectives: Talk about insects that we like and how we can take care of them.

Unit 6 — Why is food important?

- Circle the food that isn't healthy.

Listen and match. 🎧 95

Literacy

💡 Learning to Know

Think!
What food don't you like?

142   Unit 6

Objectives: Listen to a poem about meals at different times of the day and answer questions.

Connect the *g* words to reach the gate.

Phonemic Awareness

Learning to Know

g

Unit 6

Objectives: Identify and say words with the initial /g/ sound.

143

● **Point. Say and write.**

Mathematical Thinking — Learning to Know

7 8 ☐ 10 11 ☐ 13 14

24 25 ☐ 27 28 29 ☐ 31

37 ☐ 39 40 41 ☐ 43

45 46 ☐ 48 49 ☐

Objectives: Identify and write missing numbers to 50.

Listen and color.

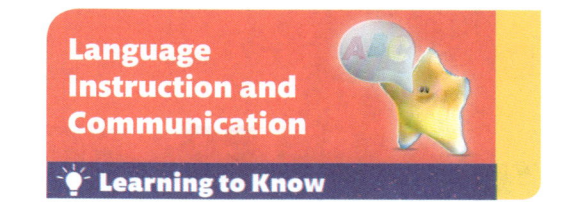

Language Instruction and Communication

Learning to Know

Objectives: Use target language to talk about different meals during the day and what we eat.

Unit 6

145

- **Circle sweet food blue. Circle salty food red.**

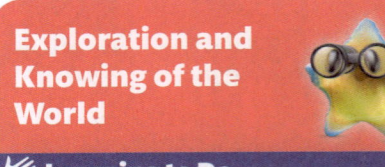

- **Mark the food you like.** ✓

Think! Are carrots sweet or salty?

146 Unit 6

Objectives: Classify food as sweet or salty.

● **Listen and circle.**

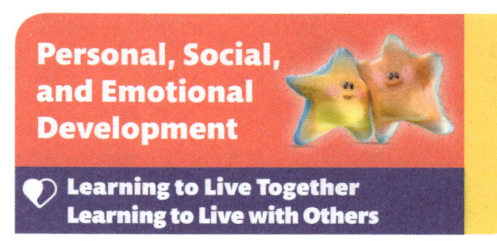

○ ○ ○ ○

● **Cut and paste.**

Objectives: Learn why it is important to be polite during meals.

Unit 6

147

- **Listen and trace.**

Sunday

Monday

Tuesday

Thursday

Wednesday

Friday

Saturday

Literacy
Learning to Know

Think!
Do you eat the same thing every day?

Unit 6

Objectives: Listen to a dialogue about favorite foods and answer questions.

Listen. Color and say the h words. Trace.

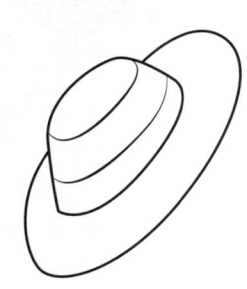

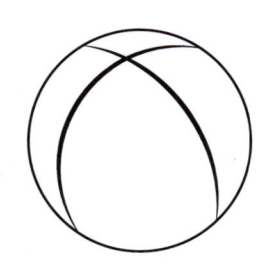

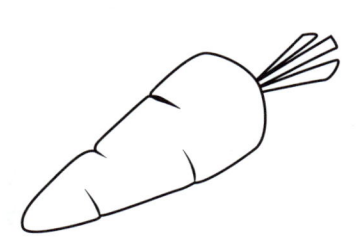

Phonemic Awareness

Learning to Know

Unit 6

Objectives: Identify and say words with the initial /h/ sound.

- **Cut and paste.**

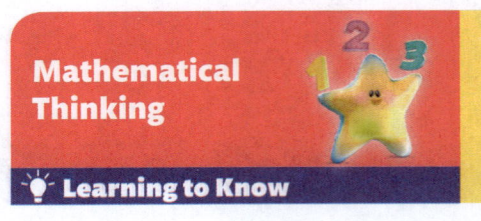

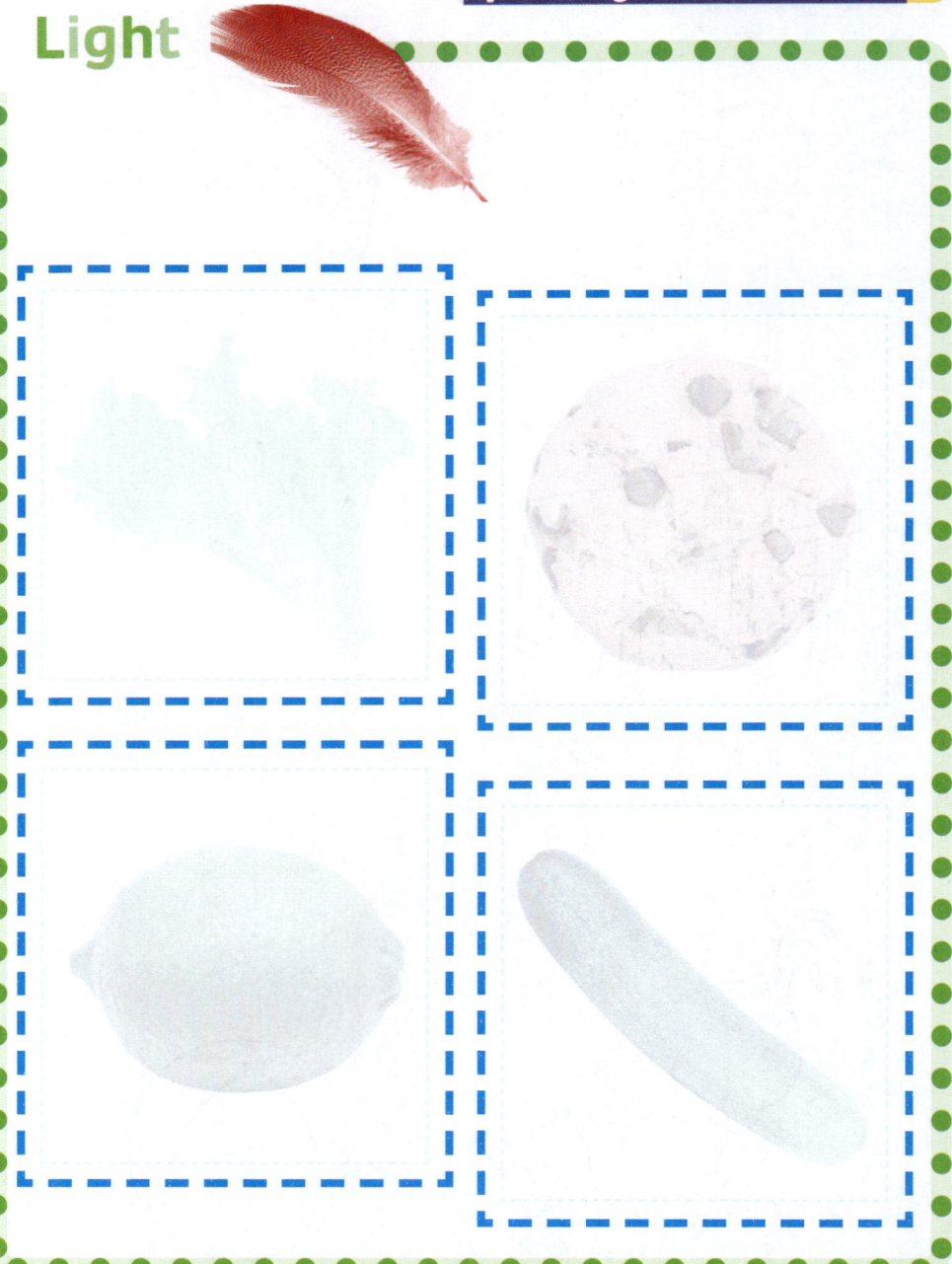

Heavy

Light

Mathematical Thinking
Learning to Know

150 Unit 6

Objectives: Use words to measure mass.

Listen and match. 🎧 101

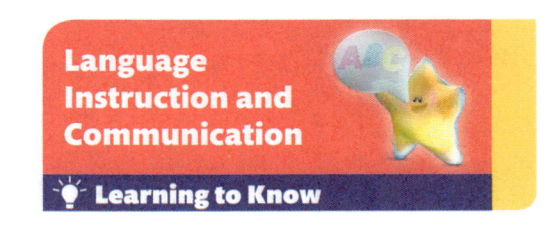

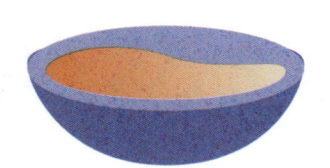

Language Instruction and Communication

Learning to Know

Unit 6

Objectives: Use target language to talk about what we use to eat.

151

- **Listen and number.**

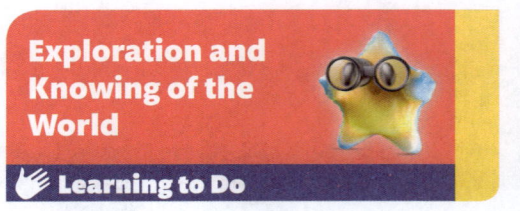

- **Draw a picture of a fruit or vegetable.**

Think!
Does a square melon taste the same as a round melon?

Unit 6

Objectives: Learn about fruit and vegetables grown in different countries.

- **Circle the spoons. Listen and say what the children do after lunch.**

- **Where do you keep your spoons?**

Objectives: Learn to take care of personal belongings including eating utensils.

Listen and circle what you like to eat for each meal. 🎧 104 ✏️

Literacy

💡 Learning to Know

Think!
Does everyone like ice cream?

154 Unit 6

Objectives: Listen to, understand, and sing a song about meals and the food we eat.

Listen. Circle the things that begin with *j*. Trace.

Phonemic Awareness

Learning to Know

Objectives: Identify and say words with the initial /j/ sound.

Unit 6

155

- **Color the groups with more objects.**

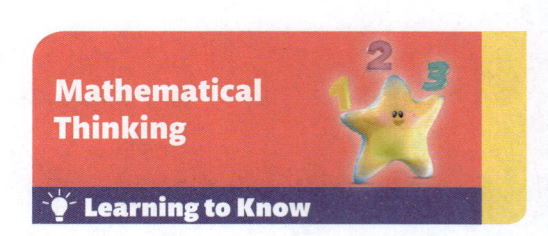

Mathematical Thinking
Learning to Know

156 Unit 6

Objectives: Identify objects in a set (more/fewer).

● **Listen and check what happens if we eat healthy food.** 🎧 106 ✓

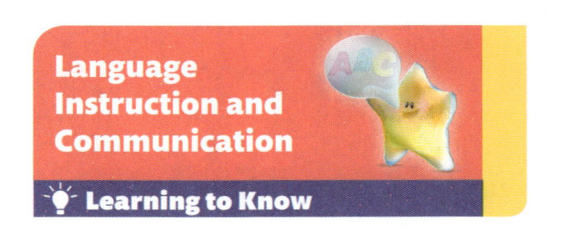

Language Instruction and Communication
💡 Learning to Know

● **Think and color the healthy food blue.**

Objectives: Use target language to talk about why healthy food is important and which snacks are not good for us.

Unit 6

157

● **Look and match.**

Exploration and Knowing of the World

Learning to Do

Think!
Are all tomatoes red?

Objectives: Experiment by cutting open different types of fruit and vegetables and finding symmetrical shapes.

158 Unit 6

Listen and trace.

Personal, Social, and Emotional Development

Learning to Live Together
Learning to Live with Others

Think! Why do we need to eat clean vegetables?

Objectives: Learn why it is important to wash fruit and vegetables before you eat them.

Unit 6

159

- **Listen. What are the children's problems?** 🎧 108

- **Listen again and act out.** 🎧 108

Literacy
Learning to Know

Unit 6

Objectives: Listen to a story about the utensils we use to eat and retell it.

Listen. Color and say the *k* words. Trace. 🎧 109 ✏️ 👄

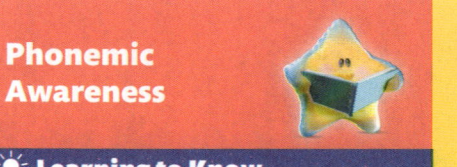

Phonemic Awareness

💡 Learning to Know

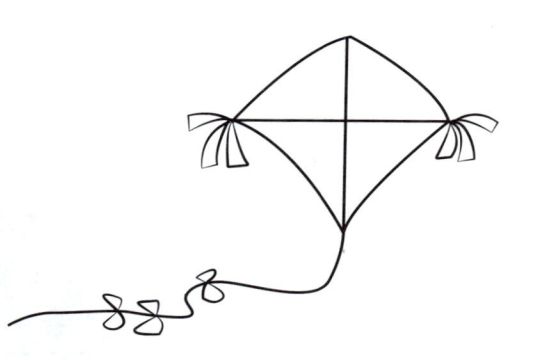

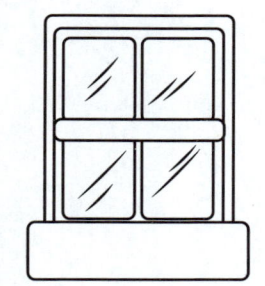

Objectives: Identify and say words with the initial /k/ sound.

Unit 6

● **Use triangles. Fill in the shapes with triangles.**

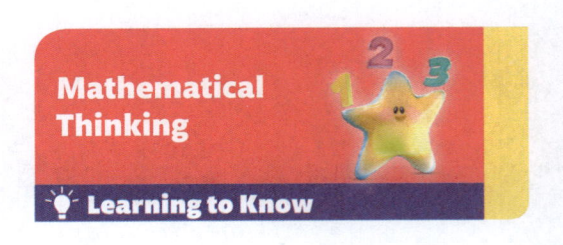

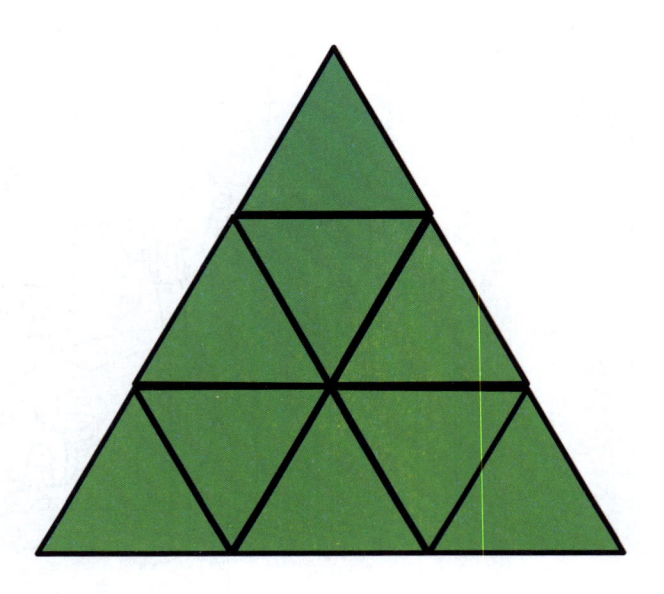

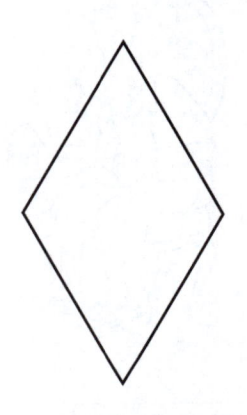

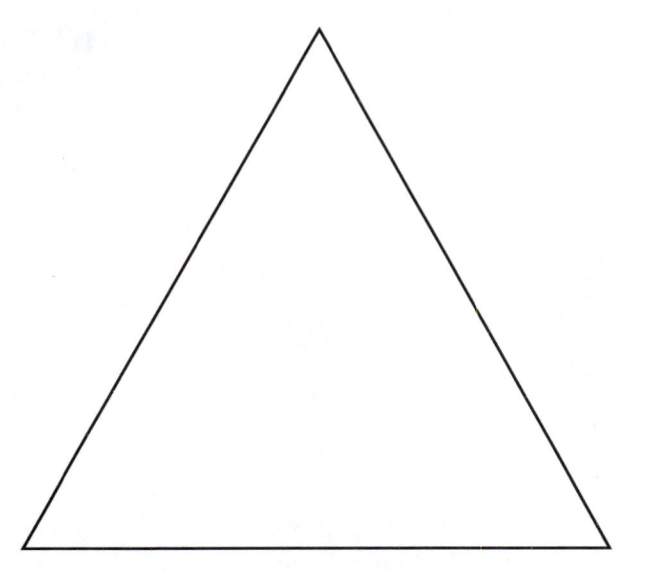

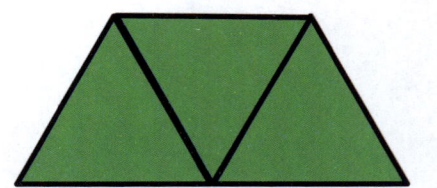

Mathematical Thinking
Learning to Know

Objectives: Use shapes to make other shapes.

Listen and draw.

What's your favorite food?

Objectives: Use target language to talk about our favorite food.

Unit 6

163

● **Count the seeds and match.**

1   2   3   4   5

Think!
What happens if you plant a seed?

Exploration and Knowing of the World
Learning to Do

Unit 6

Objectives: Count the number of seeds found in different types of fruit and record findings.

● **Look and number.**

Personal, Social, and Emotional Development

Learning to Live Together
Learning to Live with Others

Think!
How many times do you wash your hands every day?

● **Listen and act out.**

Objectives: Remember why it's important to wash your hands before meals.

Unit 6

165

Listen and circle the food the girl likes. 🎧 112 ✏️

Literacy

💡 Learning to Know

166 Unit 6

Objectives: Listen to and retell a story about lunch.

- **Draw a word that begins with *g* and one with *h*. Trace. Say.**

Phonemic Awareness — Learning to Know

g

h

Objectives: Identify and say words with the initial /g/ and /h/ sounds.

Unit 6

- **Count and color one more.**

0 1 2 3 4 5 6 7 8 9 10

4 + 1 = 5

6 + 1 = 7

2 + 1 = 3

9 + 1 = 10

- **Write.**

7 + 1 =

5 + 1 =

8 + 1 =

☐ + ☐ = ☐

168 Unit 6

Objectives: Add one to a number.

- **Listen and match.** 🎧

- **Draw and say what's in your lunchbox.** ✏️👄

Objectives: Use target language to talk about the food in their lunchbox.

Unit 6

- **Cut out and paste pictures of spicy or sour food.**

Spicy

Sour

Think!
Did you eat something spicy today?

Unit 6

Objectives: Classify food as spicy or sour.

- **Listen and check the child that eats the better lunch.** 🎧 115 ✓

Personal, Social, and Emotional Development

Learning to Live Together
Learning to Live with Others

Objectives: Talk about why it is important to eat a healthy school lunch.

Unit 6   171

Listen and color the snack.

Literacy

💡 Learning to Know

172　Unit 6

Objectives: Listen to and retell a story about following a recipe for a healthy snack.

● **Listen. Match the pictures to a *j* or a *k* sound. Say. Color.** 🎧117 👄 ✏️

Phonemic Awareness

💡 Learning to Know

Objectives: Identify and say words with the initial /j/ and /k/ sounds.

Unit 6

173

Point. Name. Cut. Paste.

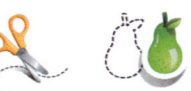

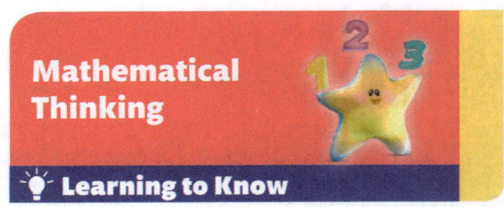

Sour

Spicy

174 Unit 6

Objectives: Classify food.

- **Draw a healthy snack you like.**

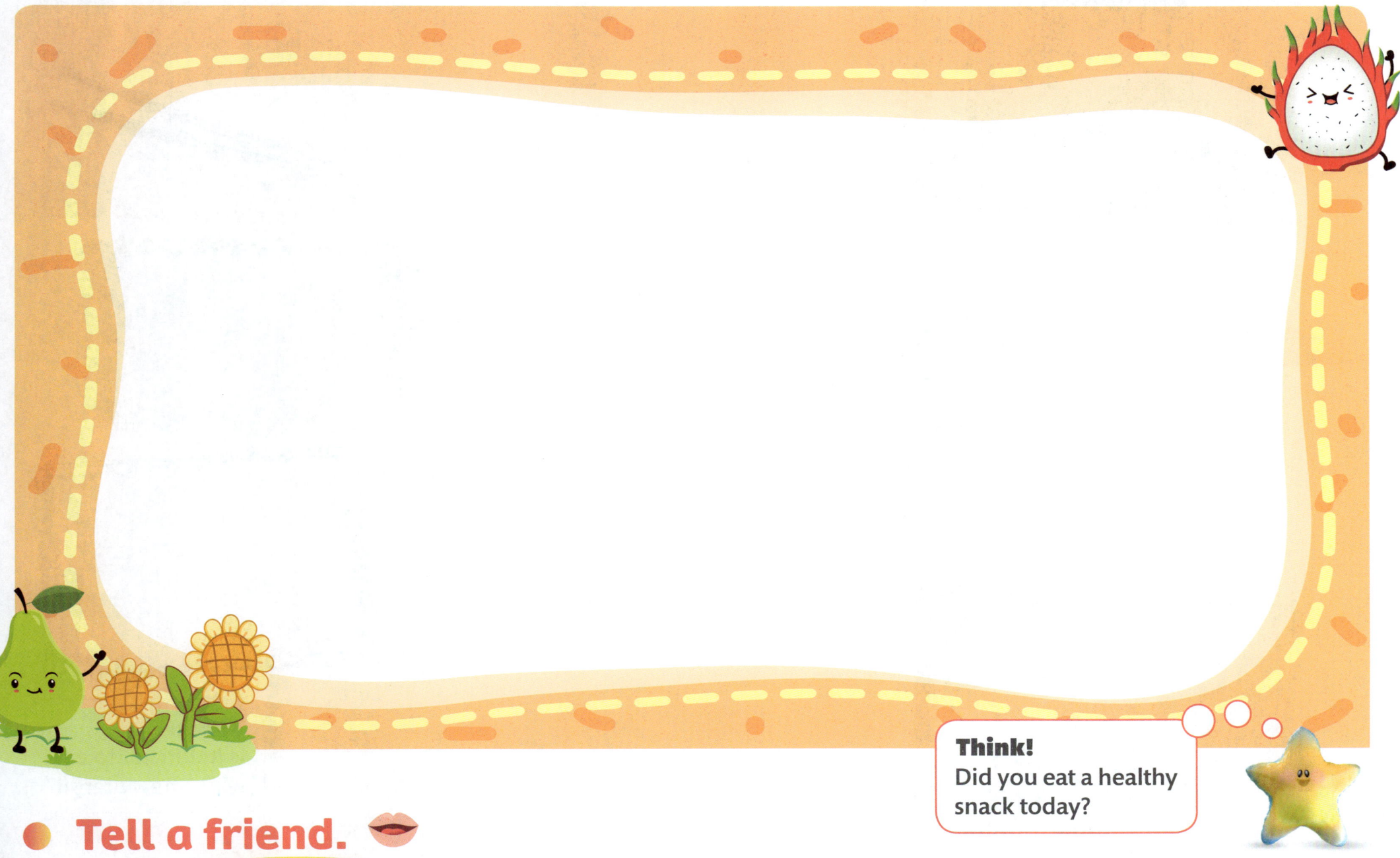

- **Tell a friend.**

Think!
Did you eat a healthy snack today?

Objectives: Use target language to talk about the preparation of a healthy snack.

Language Instruction and Communication

Learning to Know

Unit 6

● **Listen and match.** 🎧 118

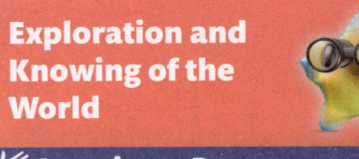

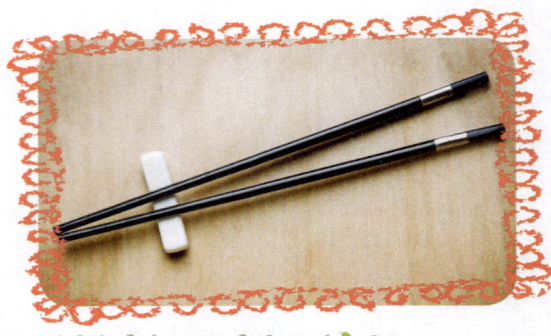

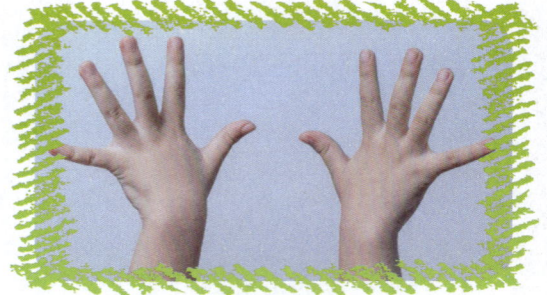

Exploration and Knowing of the World

☞ Learning to Do

Think!
Is it difficult to eat with a new utensil?

176　Unit 6

Objectives: Learn about the utensils people from other countries use to eat.

Listen and number.

Personal, Social, and Emotional Development

Learning to Live Together
Learning to Live with Others

Objectives: Learn about sharing food with others.

Unit 6

177

Unit 7 How can farm animals help us?

- Look and say. Which animals do you know?

- Listen and sing.

- **Listen and sing. Circle the animal that goes "quack."** 🎧 122 👄 ✏️

Literacy

💡 Learning to Know

Think! What noise do these animals make in your language?

Objectives: Listen to, understand, and sing a song about farm animals and the sounds they make.

Unit 7

- **Listen. Color the pictures that begin with *w*. Trace.**

180 Unit 7

Objectives: Identify and say words with the initial /w/ sound.

Phonemic Awareness
Learning to Know

- **Count and color to make ten. Write.**

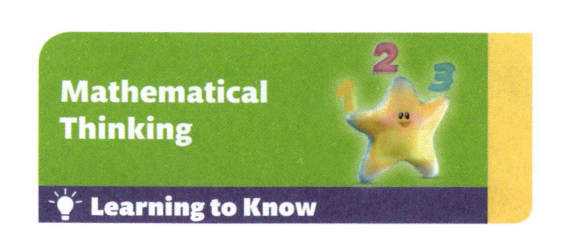

0 1 2 3 4 5 6 7 8 9 10 11 12 13 14 15 16 17 18 19 20

4 + 6 = 10

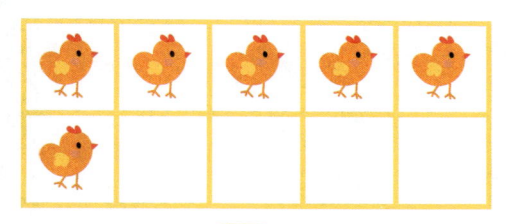

6 + 4 = 10

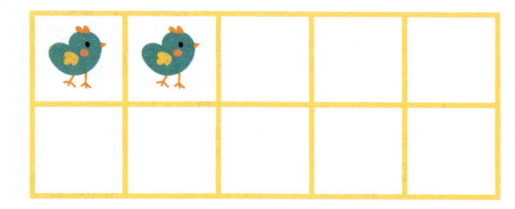

2 + 8 = 10

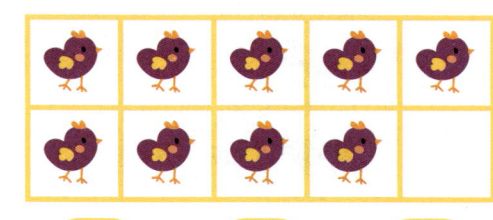

9 + 1 = 10

- **Draw.**

7 + 3 = 10

3 + 7 = 10

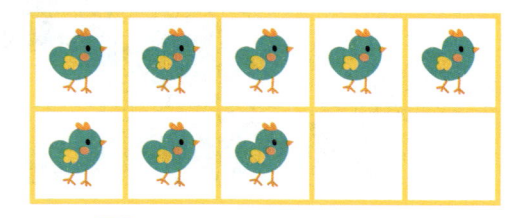

8 + 2 = 10

☐ + ☐ = ☐

Objectives: Begin to add to ten.

Unit 7

● **Listen and number.**

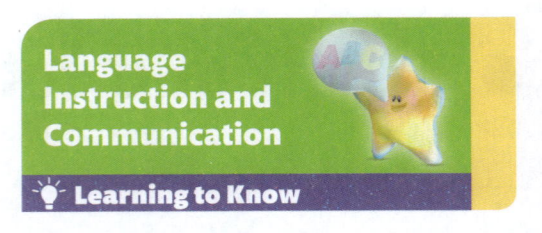

● **Say which sound the animals make.**

182 Unit 7

Objectives: Use target language to talk about farm animals and the sounds they make.

- **Look and match.**

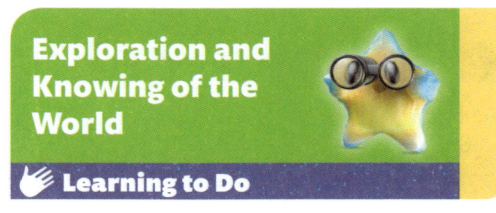

Exploration and Knowing of the World
Learning to Do

- **Circle the products you eat or drink.**

Think! Do cows give us eggs?

Unit 7

Objectives: Identify the farm animal some food comes from.

- **Listen, cut, and paste.** 🎧 125 ✂️

- **Say which sound the animals make.** 👄

184 Unit 7

Personal, Social, and Emotional Development

Learning to Live Together
Learning to Live with Others

Objectives: Learn how farm animals help us.

- **Listen and follow.** 🎧 126

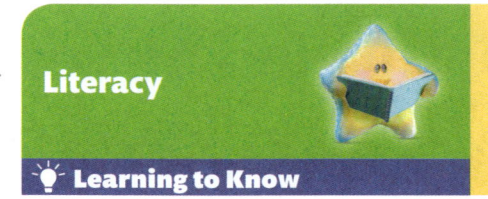

  Literacy
  💡 Learning to Know

- **Look and say where the animals are.** 👁 👄

Objectives: Listen to and retell a story about farm animals.

Unit 7 185

● **Circle the words that begin with a *v* sound and say. Trace.**

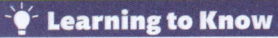

Phonemic Awareness
Learning to Know

Objectives: Identify and say words with the initial /v/ sound.

Count and color.

Mathematical Thinking

Learning to Know

Objectives: Make a simple bar graph.

Unit 7

● Listen and match. 🎧 128

Language Instruction and Communication

💡 Learning to Know

188 Unit 7

Objectives: Use target language to talk about farm animals and their babies.

Listen and draw the animal you hear. 🎧 129 ✏️

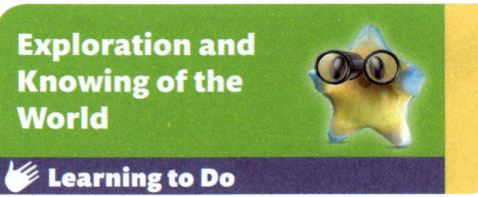

Exploration and Knowing of the World

👏 Learning to Do

Think!
What noise do babies make?

Objectives: Identify different animal sounds and match them to the corresponding animal.

Unit 7

Listen and match.

Personal, Social, and Emotional Development

Learning to Live Together
Learning to Live with Others

Think!
Can you think of something that lambs don't need that babies do need?

190   Unit 7

Objectives: Talk about treating farm animals with respect.

Listen and color the animals with horns.

Objectives: Listen to and understand a dialogue about farm animals and their characteristics.

Literacy

Learning to Know

Unit 7

191

- **Listen. Connect the pictures that begin with *y*. Follow the yarn. Trace.**

Phonemic Awareness
Learning to Know

192 Unit 7

Objectives: Identify and say words with the initial /y/ sound.

- **Look at your 50 chart. Write the numbers.**

| 36 | 37 | 38 |

| | 25 | |

| | 12 | |

| 8 | 9 | 10 |

| | 40 | 41 |

| 27 | 28 | |

Mathematical Thinking — Learning to Know

Objectives: Identify missing numbers on a 50 chart.

Unit 7

● Listen and match. 🎧

Language Instruction and Communication
💡 Learning to Know

194 Unit 7

Objectives: Use target language to identify animal body parts and match them.

Listen and number.

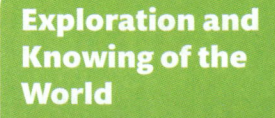

Exploration and Knowing of the World

Learning to Do

Think! Which animal has only two legs?

Objectives: Learn about unusual farm animals.

Unit 7

195

- **Listen and check how chickens take care of their babies.** 🎧 135 ✏️

Personal, Social, and Emotional Development

♥ Learning to Live Together
Learning to Live with Others

Think!
Can you curl up like you are inside an egg?

196 Unit 7

Objectives: Learn about how chickens take care of their babies.

- **Listen and say. Where is the lamb? Where is the chick?** 🎧 👄

Literacy
💡 Learning to Know

- **Act out.** 👄

Objectives: Listen to a poem about farm animals and answer questions.

Unit 7

● Listen and match. 🎧 137

W

y

v

198 Unit 7

Phonemic Awareness
💡 Learning to Know

Objectives: Identify and say words with the initial /w/, /v/, and /y/ sounds.

Listen and draw.

Mathematical Thinking

Learning to Know

Objectives: Identify position and location.

Unit 7

Listen and circle what each animal eats. 🎧 138 ✏️

Language Instruction and Communication
💡 Learning to Know

200 Unit 7

Objectives: Use target language to talk about what farm animals eat.

Look and cross out.

Exploration and Knowing of the World

Learning to Do

Think! Do people have fur?

Objectives: Classify animals according to their physical characteristics.

Unit 7

201

● Listen and follow. 🎧 139

Personal, Social, and Emotional Development
Learning to Live Together
Learning to Live with Others

● Draw a healthy foal. ✏️

202   Unit 7

Objectives: Learn about how horses take care of their babies.

Unit 8 — Who lives and works in my town?

- **Listen. Look and check.** 🎧141 👁 ✔

- **Listen and sing.** 🎧141 👄

203

Listen and color. 🎧 142

Literacy

Learning to Know

Think!
Did you see a doctor today?

204 Unit 8

Objectives: Listen to and understand a story about people in the community and the jobs they do.

- **Draw a queen and a question mark. Trace.**

Phonemic Awareness
Learning to Know

q

Objectives: Identify words with the initial /q/ sound.

Unit 8

205

- **Look at your 50 chart. Write the numbers.**

| 20 | 21 | 22 |

| | 19 | |

| | 37 | |

| | 44 | |

| | 26 | |

| | 30 | |

Objectives: Identify numbers before and after using a 50 chart.

● **Listen and point.** 🎧 144

Language Instruction and Communication
💡 Learning to Know

● **Match and say what the people do.**

Objectives: Use target language to talk about the jobs that people do in the community.

Unit 8 **207**

Listen and trace.

Exploration and Knowing of the World

Learning to Do

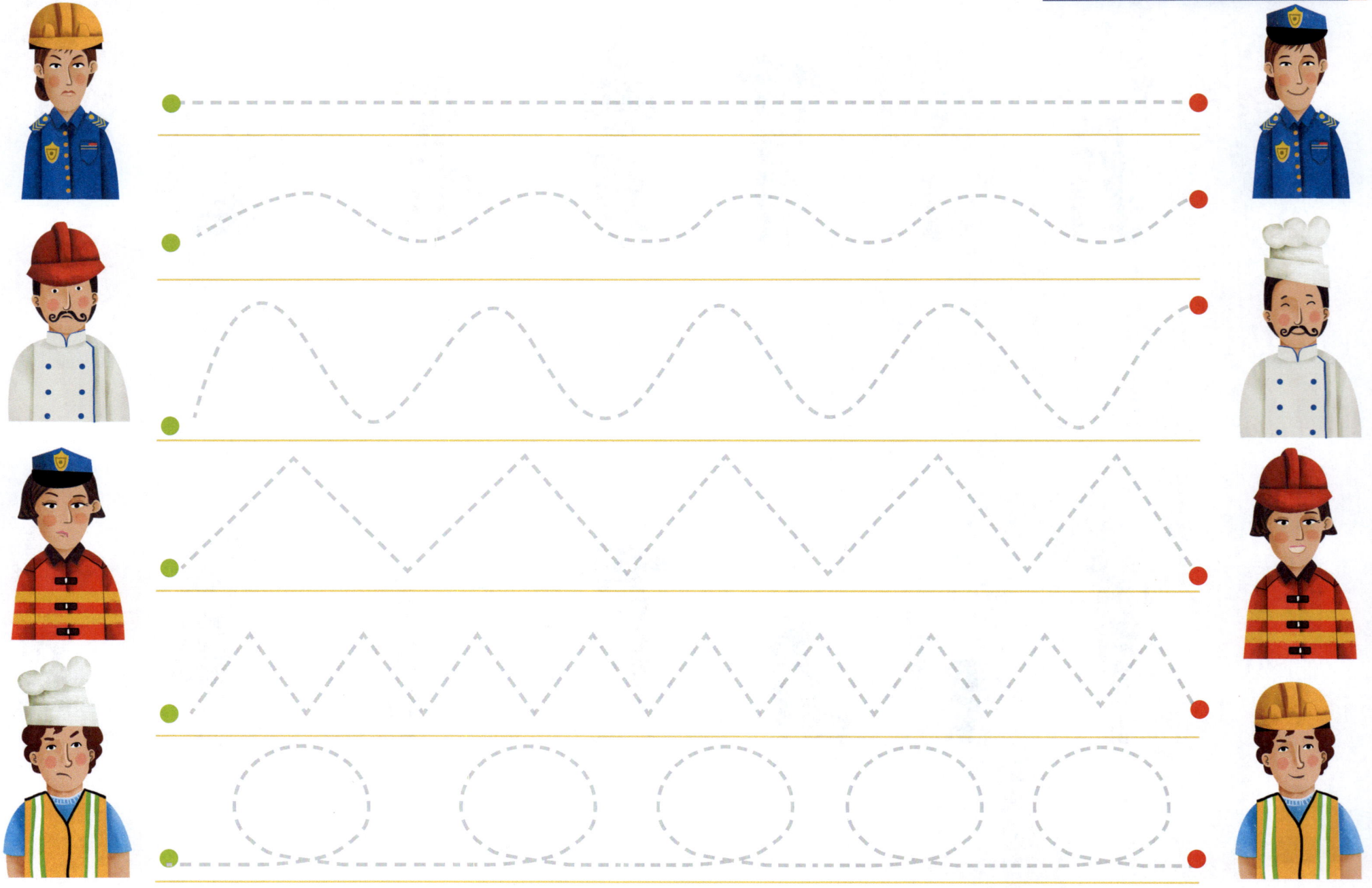

208 Unit 8

Objectives: Identify uniforms and match to the community workers.

- **Talk about people you know who do these jobs.**

- **Draw.**

Objectives: Compare knowledge about community workers with classmates and respect different opinions.

Language Instruction and Communication
Learning to Know

Unit 8

Listen and number.

Literacy

Learning to Know

Think!
How do you help your community?

Objectives: Listen to and retell a story about community workers and how they help people.

210 Unit 8

● **Listen. Circle the pictures with an *x* sound. Say.**

x

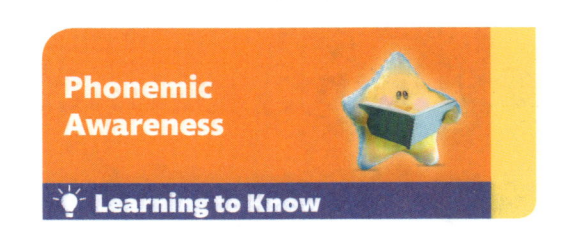

Objectives: Identify words with the /x/ sound.

Phonemic Awareness

Learning to Know

Unit 8

211

- **Point, count, and color.**

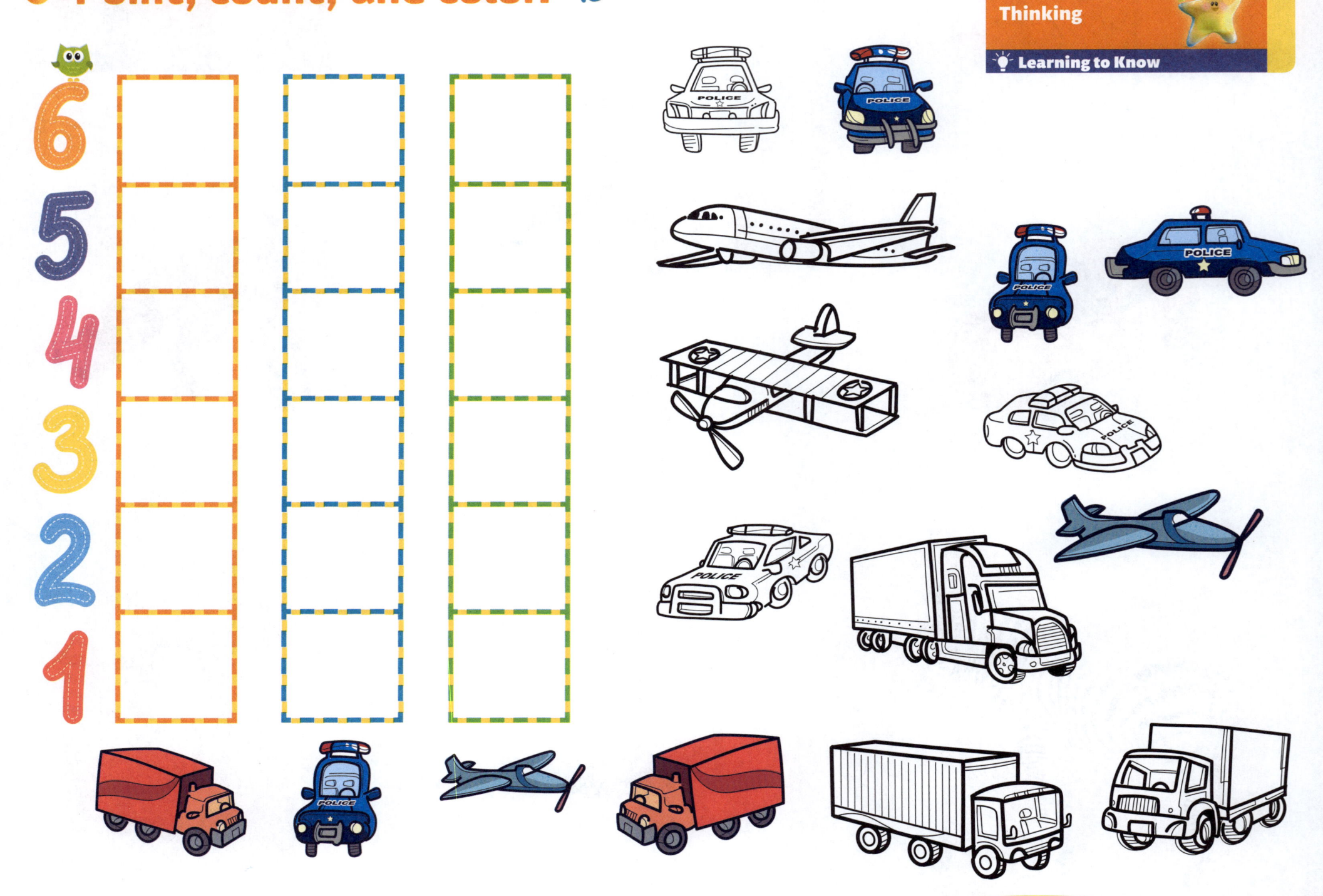

6
5
4
3
2
1

Mathematical Thinking

Learning to Know

212 Unit 8

Objectives: Make a simple bar graph.

Listen and point. Say. Color. 🎧 👄 ✏️

Language Instruction and Communication

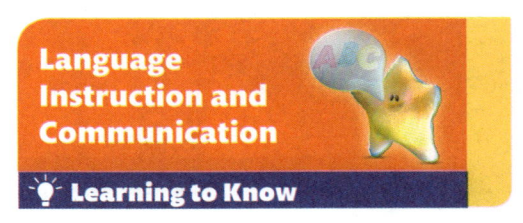

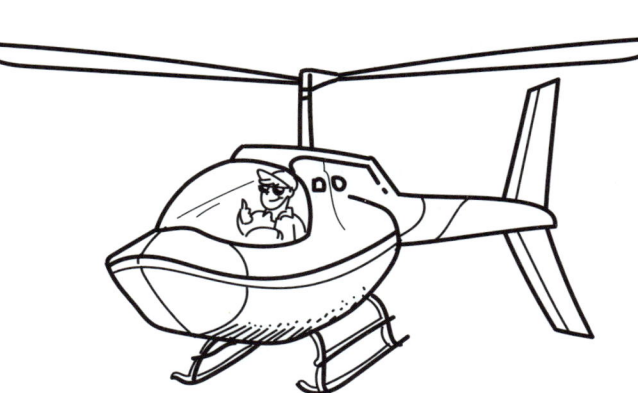

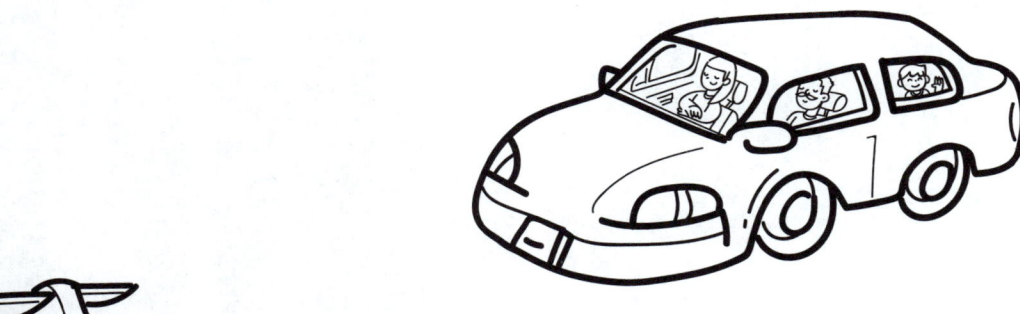

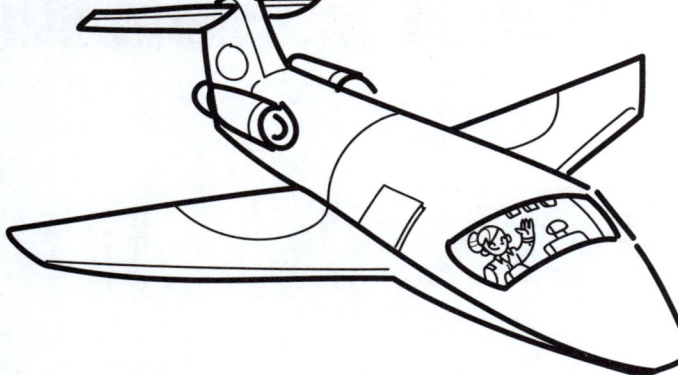

💡 Learning to Know

Think!
Which form of transportation do you use?

Objectives: Use target language to talk about transportation and what people use in the community.

Unit 8

213

- **Listen and match.** 🎧 149

Exploration and Knowing of the World

Learning to Do

214　Unit 8

Objectives: Learn about firefighters and construction workers.

● Listen and number.

Personal, Social, and Emotional Development
♥ Learning to Live Together
Learning to Live with Others

Objectives: Role-play how nurses and doctors can help you when you are sick.

Unit 8   **215**

Listen and circle.

Literacy

Learning to Know

Think!
Do you know what you want to be?

Objectives: Listen to a poem about jobs and answer questions.

- **Listen. Follow the zipper, say the words. Trace.**

zoo

z

Phonemic Awareness

Learning to Know

Objectives: Identify words with the initial /z/ sound.

Unit 8   217

- **Color the shorter object.**

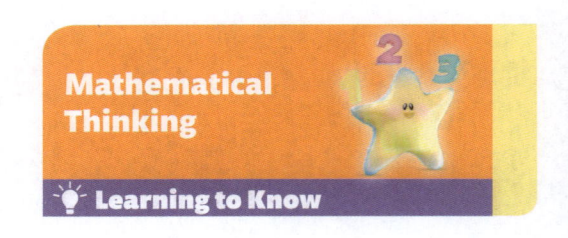

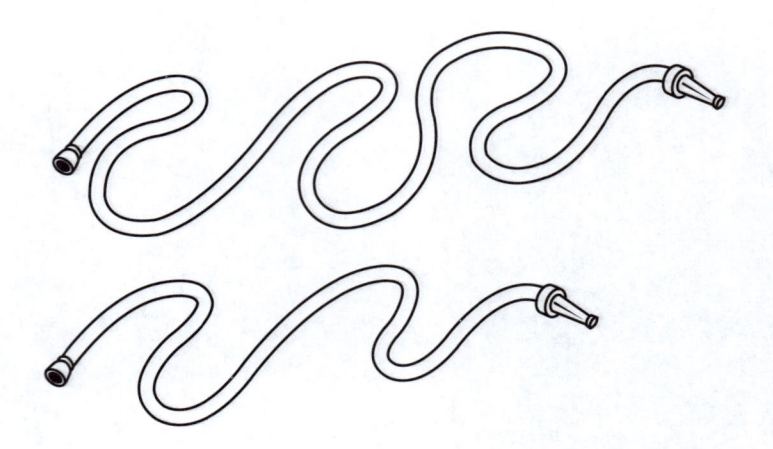

- **Color the longer object.**

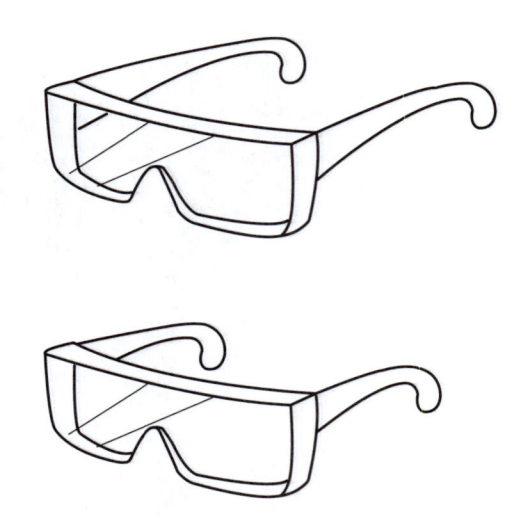

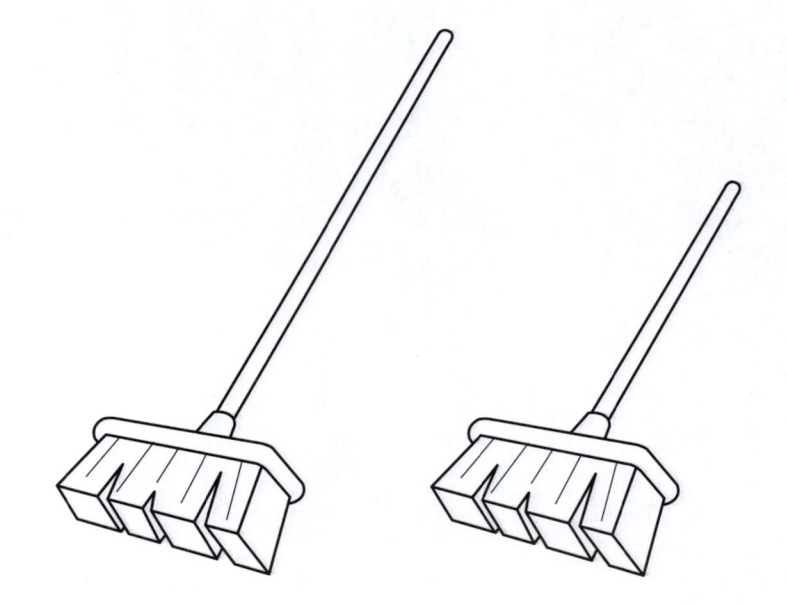

218 unit 8

Objectives: Identify longer and shorter objects.

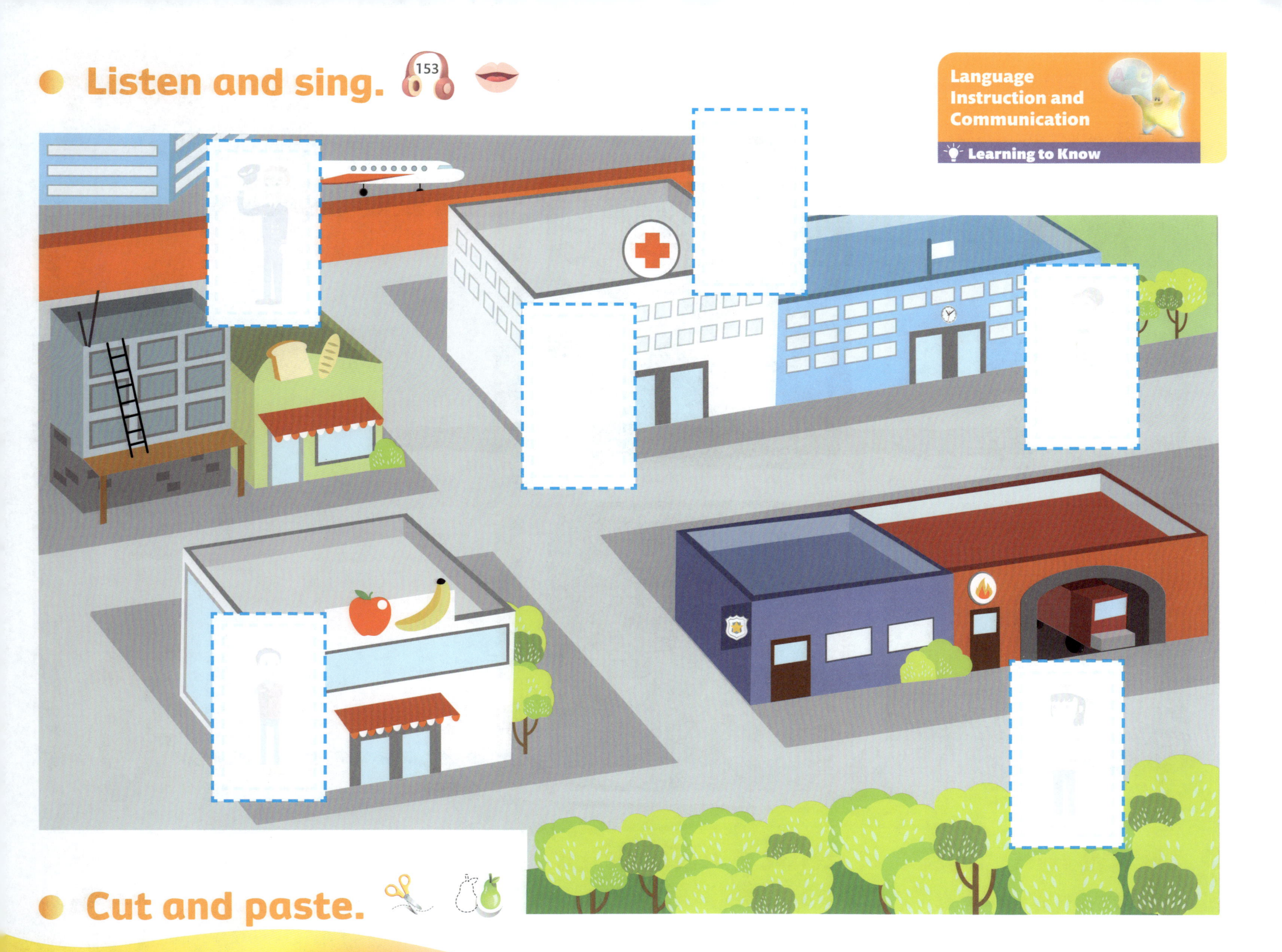

Listen and sing.

Language Instruction and Communication
Learning to Know

Cut and paste.

Objectives: Use target language to talk about where community workers work in town.

Unit 8

219

- **Look and say what color the uniforms are.**

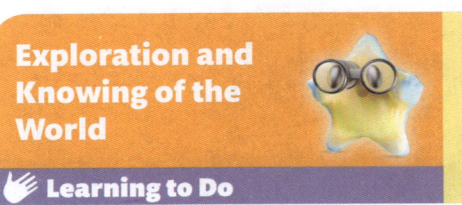

Exploration and Knowing of the World

Learning to Do

- **Draw and color a police officer or a firefighter from your country.**

Unit 8

Objectives: Learn about different community workers from around the world and the jobs they do.

- **Listen and check.** 🎧 154 ✓

Personal, Social, and Emotional Development

Learning to Live Together
Learning to Live with Others

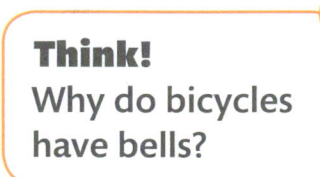

Think!
Why do bicycles have bells?

Objectives: Learn about road traffic safety in your town.

Unit 8

221

● **Listen and sing. Check.** 🎧 155 👄 ✔

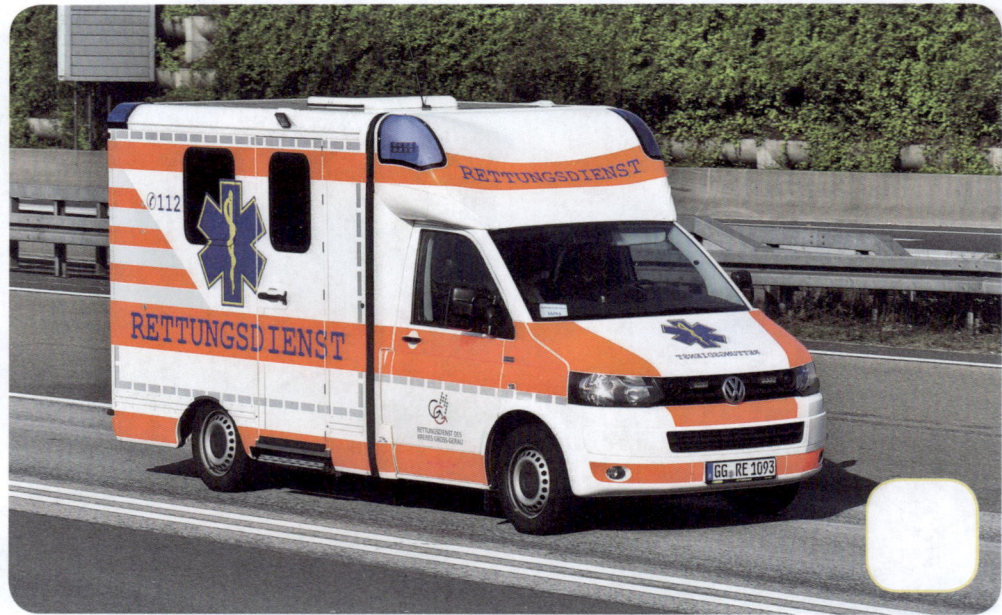

Literacy

Learning to Know

222 Unit 8

Objectives: Listen to, understand, and sing a song about some community workers and the transportation they use.

Look at the pictures and write the sounds.

Phonemic Awareness
Learning to Know

Objectives: Identify words with /q/, /x/, and /z/ sounds.

Unit 8   **223**

- **Think. Draw and write.**

I like to do this during math time:

Mathematical Thinking
Learning to Know

Objectives: Illustrate favorite math activities.

- **Look and draw to complete the picture.**

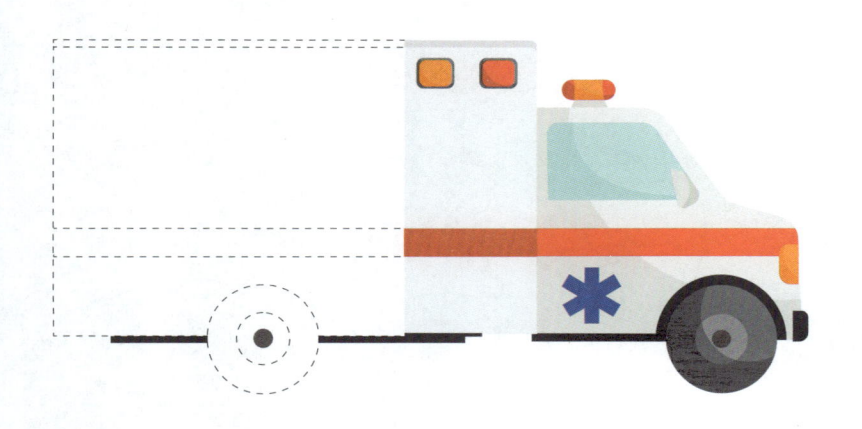

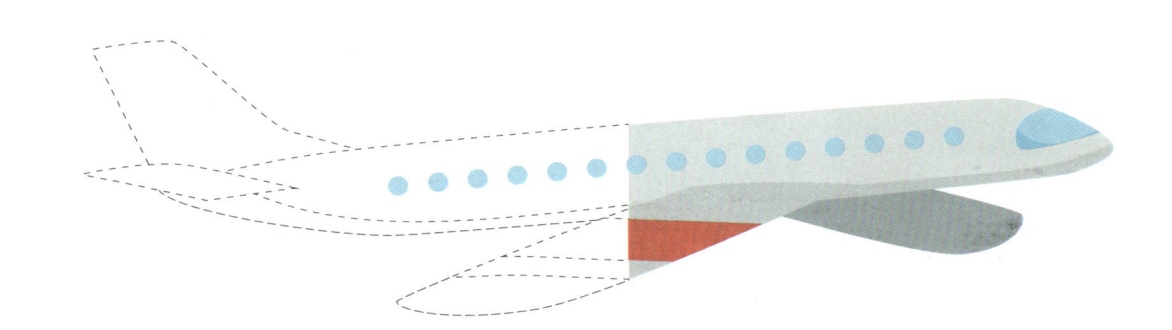

- **Say who uses each type of transportation and role-play.**

Objectives: Use target language to talk about community workers and the transportation they use.

Language Instruction and Communication

Learning to Know

Unit 8

● **Listen and check. What should you do if you feel sick?** 🎧157 ✅

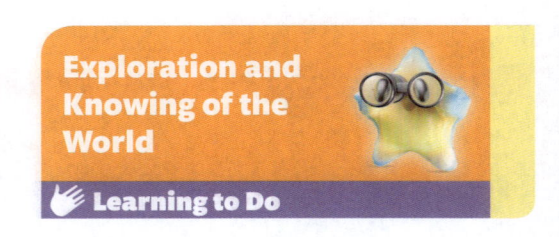

Exploration and Knowing of the World

Learning to Do

226 Unit 8

Objectives: Learn about how to take care of ourselves when we are sick.

- **Look. Check the correct action and cross out the incorrect action. Say.**

Personal, Social, and Emotional Development
Learning to Live Together
Learning to Live with Others

Think!
Do you obey rules?

Objectives: Learn about rules in your town and why it is important to respect them.

Unit 8

227

Unit 2, page 53

Unit 1, page 26

Unit 3, page 65

229

Unit 6, page 150

Unit 4, page 92

Unit 6, page 147

Unit 5, page 132

231

Unit 7, page 184

Unit 8, page 219

Unit 6, page 174

233

Mathematical Thinking, Pattern Blocks

Mathematical Thinking, Pattern Blocks

237

Mathematical Thinking, Pattern Blocks

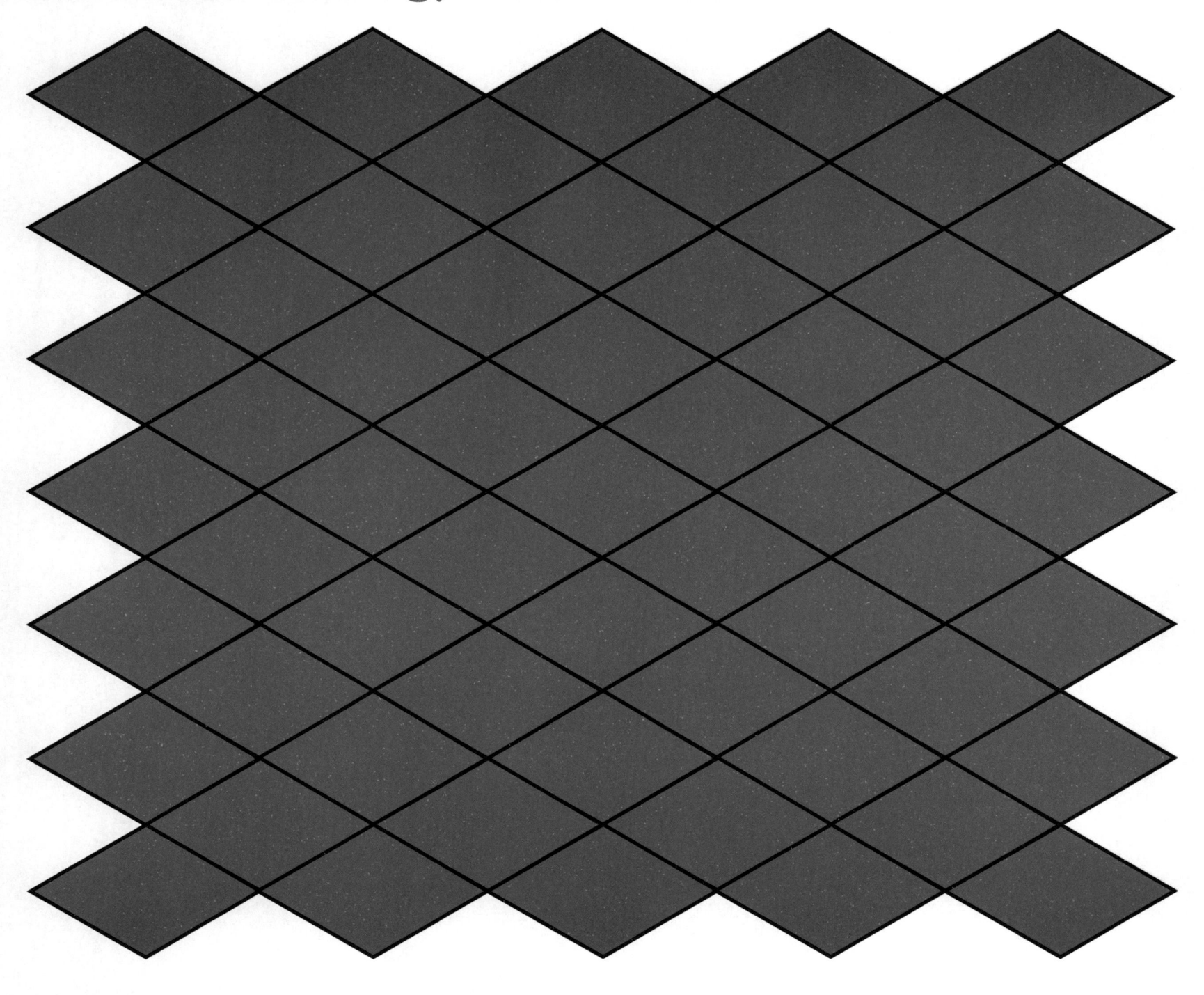

239

Mathematical Thinking, Pattern Blocks

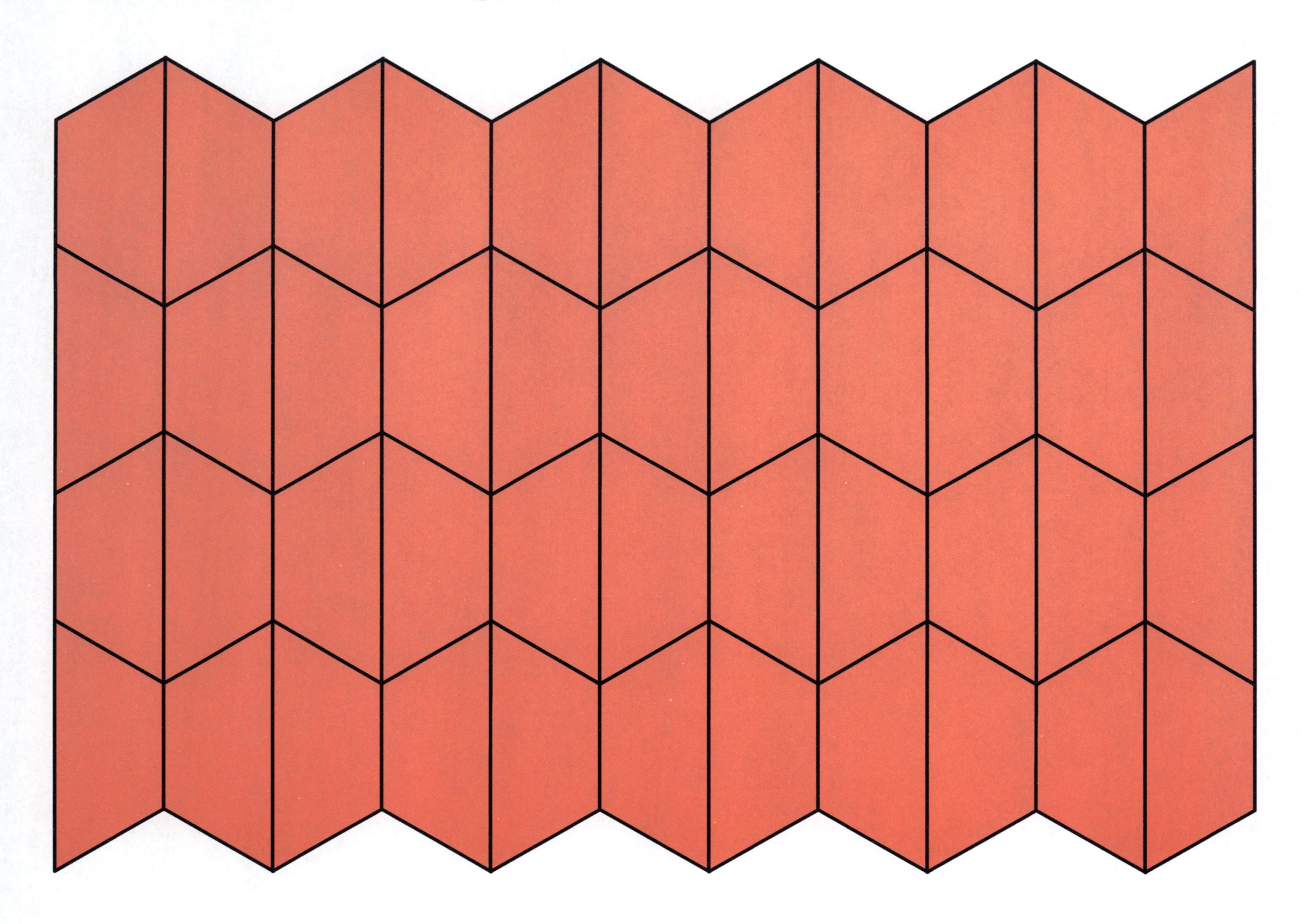

Mathematical Thinking, Pattern Blocks

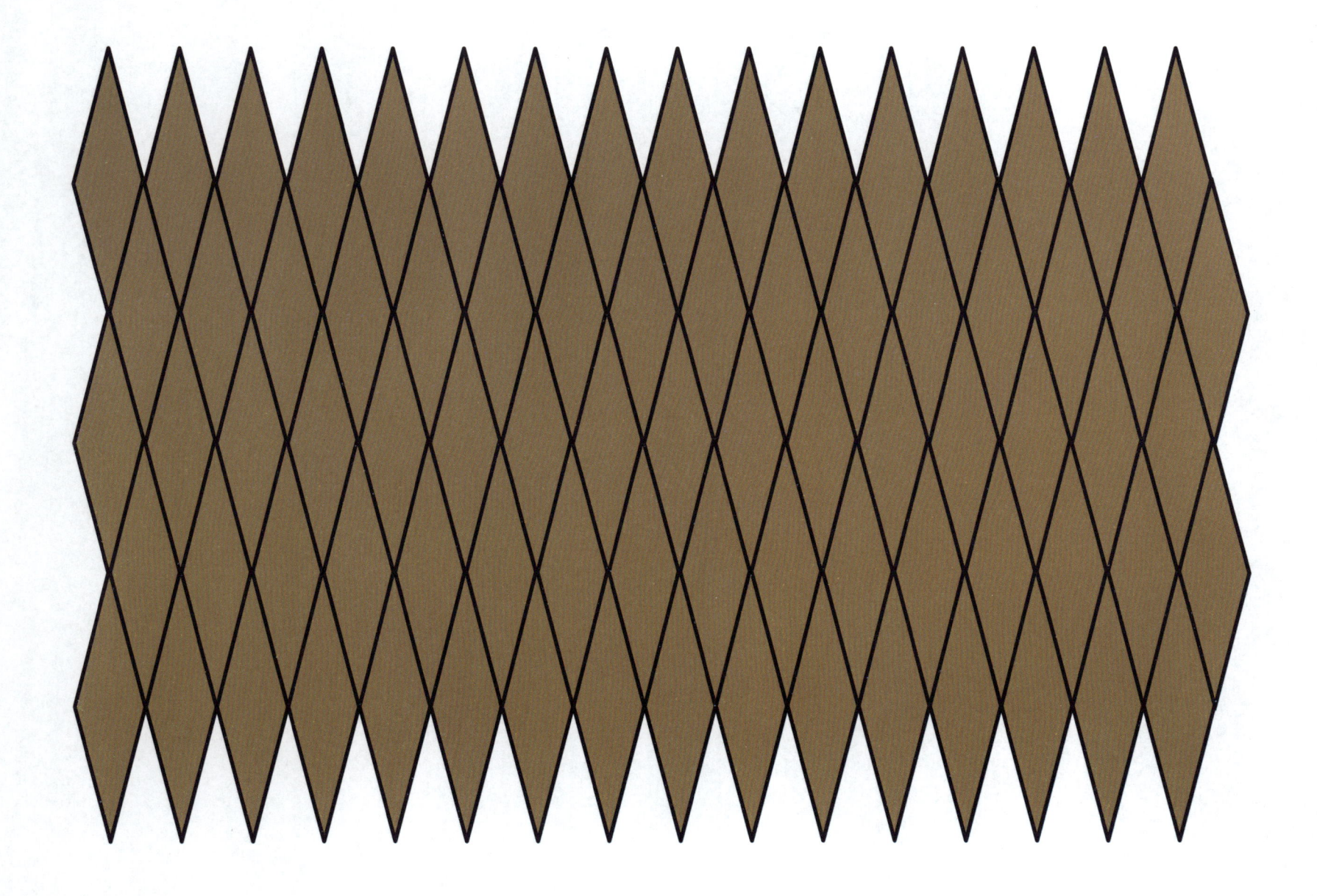

Mathematical Thinking, Pattern Blocks

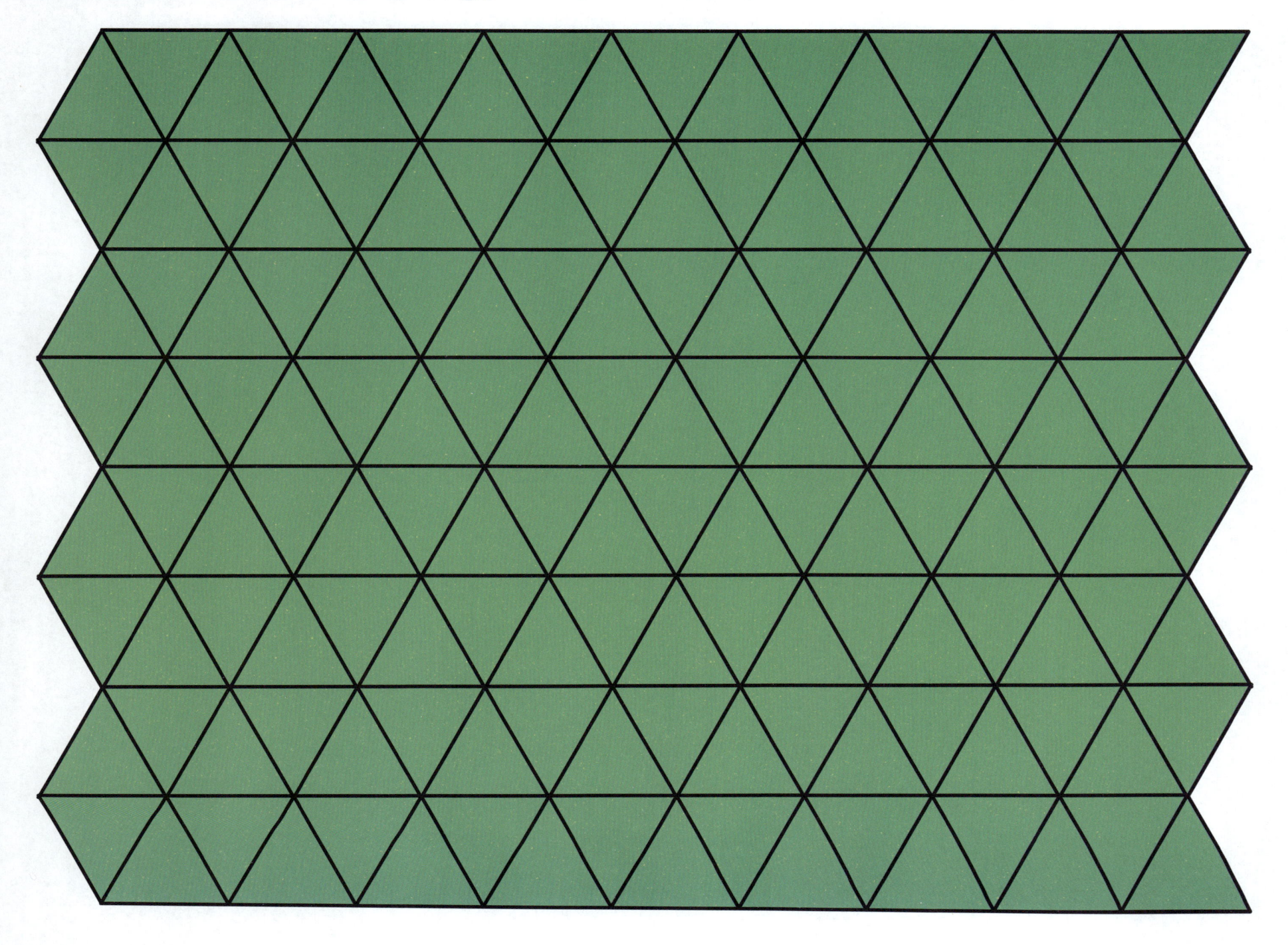

My Starfish 50 Chart

1	2	3	4	5	6	7	8	9	10
11	12	13	14	15	16	17	18	19	20
21	22	23	24	25	26	27	28	29	30
31	32	33	34	35	36	37	38	39	40
41	42	43	44	45	46	47	48	49	50